ON YOUR OWN TWO FEET

ON YOUR OWN TWO FEET

How to Use *Natural Law* to Avoid Burnout and Ensure Business Success

Dr Therese Perdedjian

Art of Chiropractic

Art of Chiropractic

Published By The Art of Chiropractic Studio
www.artofchiropractic.com.au

For quantity sales or media enquires, please contact the publisher at the website address above.

ISBN: 978-1-7637596-0-2 (paperback)
      978-1-7637596-1-9 (eBook)
      978-1-7637596-2-6 (audiobook)

Edited by Stephanie Dale
Cover designed by Julia Kuris
Typeset in Bembo and Lucida Sans by Sunset Publishing Services Pty Ltd
eBook formatted by Sunset Publishing Services Pty Ltd

A catalogue record for this book is available from the National Library of Australia

NATIONAL LIBRARY OF AUSTRALIA

Aligning your work practice with your life practice

To my mum and dad
Thank you
I love you

To all the practitioners who, with their hearts, help people.

CONTENTS

FOREWORD

When Dr Therese Perdedjian asked me to write the foreword to her first book, I asked her what her wildest desires for the book were. She wrote that the grand vision for the book was to disrupt a whole profession, to create an environment where the art of expression of authentic practice would not be feared or delayed, but would be embraced and applied; a vision to create a movement in healthcare, starting with practitioners, to produce a global collective of people proactive in their choices for health and life – thereby transforming the current form of 'healthcare' into what healthcare was actually intended to be.

Perdedjian herself initially struggled with authentic self-expression in practice, and it's not uncommon for practitioners in any modality to struggle.

On Your Own Two Feet is the culmination of Dr Perdedjian's personal and clinical experience and makes available to readers her business practice knowledge base. The book presents tips, tools and techniques for achieving what the subtitle promises: ensuring business practice success.

What strikes me about Perdedjian's book is that she understands that for any practice it is about the long haul, the long game and not the instant, gratifying emotional highs. She shares these concepts in her book as she, too, went from emotional highs and lows before committing to the long haul.

Perdedjian works with 'natural law' in her practice, and her book reflects these principles of nature. *On Your Own Two Feet* is modelled on the three primary natural law principles Perdedjian has refined in her practice:

1. The law of interconnectedness.
2. The law of correspondence (e.g., as above, so below).
3. The law of inspired action.

On Your Own Two Feet was written for practitioners questioning workplace satisfaction, who are concerned about ongoing income and who endure physical pain and injury, exhaustion and/or misalignment with the clinical practices of their employer, if they are employed.

Perdedjian writes: "It's about overcoming self-doubt, about learning to trust your style of practice, about avoiding chronic overwhelm when faced with decisions that are necessary to move a practice forward."

Perdedjian continues: "There is nothing in this book I haven't experienced myself – the highs and the lows. I wanted to share my experiences of this journey, because overwork has left many practitioners feeling as if they have forgotten what it means to be human."

The book is an insightful and engaging read, giving you comfort to know that you are not alone. It offers self-reflective and applicable exercises to help you build momentum and to give you the business success results you desire.

Dr John F. Demartini
Human Behavior Expert, Polymath and
Internationally Published Author
https://drdemartini.com/

PREFACE

Fifteen years ago, straight out of graduation, I was an associate chiropractic practitioner working in someone else's practice. I felt trapped, without flexibility. I wanted the freedom to work the way I wanted and when I wanted. I was uncomfortable as an associate. I felt pressured to persuade clients to return to the practice, not because they needed additional care but to meet numbers and targets. My discomfort meant I felt like a loser when I had low client numbers, and I felt like a fraud when I treated people back-to-back.

To top it off, I had a different style of working than the business owners. My practice principles were not traditional, and my training philosophy was innovative. I needed to find my own expression of practice, implementing what I had learned through time and experience rather than promoting practices and principles I didn't believe in. Those early years were a mixture of nervousness, self-questioning and self-exclusion, as peers did not share my professional priorities.

So I made a plan: I would gain business experience, enhance my skills, and learn from mentors before opening my own clinic. This time of transition was highly rewarding as I explored my own way. As I reflect now on this journey, I am immensely grateful for the experiences that led me to where I am now – they have led me to this, my own expression of practice in my own clinic. For all the challenges I faced and overcame, I would not have done it any other way.

This book is a how-to guide for transitioning from working for someone else's clinical practice to your own business. It shares my experiences of stepping up for myself, stepping out of corporate practice into my own practice, and moving my small business forwards, by transitioning into an office based at home. And even though I trained as a chiropractor, the information in this book is applicable to any practitioner who wants to establish a practice. Whether you work in chiropractic, massage, Bowen, reiki, homeopathy, naturopathy, acupuncture, osteopathy, skin care, child birth or death doula – all health care professionals who consult with clients will benefit from this guidebook.

This book is for practitioners who:

○ feel yourself edging towards *that* transition point
○ feel confused or overwhelmed about *how* to move your practice forwards
○ want to reignite your *why* and your purpose
○ feel divided about continuing to practise
○ need money management gems to make a profit.

Indeed, this book was inspired by practitioners I've met who were questioning their workplace satisfaction, who felt uneasy about a range of issues, including income levels, physical pain and injury, exhaustion, and/or misalignment with the clinical practices of their employer. I've spoken to practitioners who long to find their own expression of practice, who say that running away would be a better solution than showing up for work tomorrow.

For me, it is important to share my experiences of this journey, because overwork has left many of us feeling as if we have forgotten what it means to be human. So, before you take radical action, consider the most radical step of all: working for yourself, either by renting a room in an existing clinic or from your own home-based practice.

For the past 11 years, I have travelled the world teaching practitioners to give language to expressions of practice that align with their values. If you would like guidance for implementing your expression in *your own* practice, this guide is (literally) a home-coming – to yourself.

On Your Own Two Feet is a nuts and bolts guide to crossing bridges and navigating obstacles on *your* path to establishing your own practice. My principles of practice are embedded in what is called 'natural law'. In essence this means I work in harmony with forces and energies of the natural world. The entirety of the ideas and reflective exercises in this book are infused with these principles. The three primary natural law principles you'll find nested in these pages are:

o the law of interconnectedness
o the law of correspondence (for example: as above, so below)
o the law of inspired action.

I am sharing my experiences of transitioning from working under someone else's clinical practice to running my own authentic practice primarily as a way of fast-tracking or easing or guiding a transition point for you. As with all journeys, the road ahead has bridges to cross and obstacles to navigate; it has challenges to face and triumphs to celebrate; it will liberate and motivate and grow and sustain you. And I'm right here beside you to say: you've got this.

And you do. You really do.

Shall we begin?

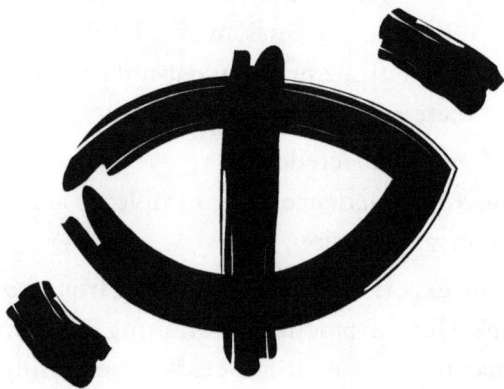

MAGIC

Magic is the word I use to describe moments in life we don't have words for, even though we know in our bones the moment is real and true. Magic moments are instances of impeccable alignment, exquisite points in a day, a month, a year, a life where things line up and we experience moments of wonder and awe. These are the moments I think 'Wow, how did I get here?' They look like magic *if* you don't understand the structures behind them. For me, the word 'magic' is a reminder that *this is a full circle moment.*

Magic is the visible, momentary expression of natural law.

Part 1: STEPPING UP

NATURAL LAW
INTERCONNECTEDNESS

1

OLD TERRITORY

There are four stories that underpin Part 1 of this book. They are: The hospital story, The migration story, The language story and The shop story. Between them, these stories illustrate the life challenges that shaped me into the practitioner I am today. The purpose of these stories is to encourage you to reflect on your own foundational stories: how has meeting and overcoming the challenges of your life provided you with the strengths and skills you need now, as you transition from a job working for others to growing a thriving authentic practice?

The hospital story

When I was five years old I visited my grandmother in hospital. At that time my family lived in Lebanon. My aunt worked at the hospital, so naturally we popped by her ward to say hello. My aunt was the head midwife and staffed the reception desk. On this particular day, positioned behind the desk, was a baby girl in a bassinet. The baby had big chunky thighs, orange hair and patches where her skin was irritated. My aunt got her milk bottle ready and asked me to feed her. She told me the baby had been abandoned outside the hospital, alone in the bassinet, and they did not know her name.

We visited the hospital a few more times that week, and each time I would feed the nameless baby behind the desk. Everyone else seemed too busy to feed the baby, so I made her my priority. On our last visit, the baby was no longer behind desk. She was gone. I remember hoping she had found her way to a loving home.

Loving and nurturing an abandoned baby left a lasting impression on my life. I felt a strong sense of responsibility for her wellbeing. In return, she made me feel like a hero. We were each other's champions. This experience ignited my desire to help people. It also sparked an awareness that I was both outsider and hero.

To this day I am the outsider who has priorities beyond the sightline of others. I see what matters and what needs doing. I champion others and genuinely seek to see people for who they are in their heart.

The migration story

It took me a while to figure out why my dad was so happy and cheerful being in Australia, away from immediate family. I remember him saying when we became Australian citizens in 1990: "Remember this day for the rest of your life. This is the best day of your life. You are now an Australian citizen."

I was born in a hospital in Lebanon. Soon after I was born, the hospital was bombed. That was the moment my parents made a life-changing decision: to eventually resettle on the other side of the world, in a small country town called Wingham, Australia. The other side of the world was exactly that – it was the other side of comfort.

The discomfort it created in me took many forms and presented many life tests. Everything I knew about life was challenged and changed, including language, family, friendships, food, and the outback. The discomforts were sudden and permeated all aspects of my life and being. I was a complete

foreigner and, at the same time, I knew it was the biggest bless-
ing for me and my family.

The standpoint of feeling foreign served me well when it
came to transitioning from working for someone else's clinical
practice to my own authentic practice. Feeling foreign was not
new to me, particularly regarding my principles and philosophy
of practice. I had been here before. *I knew it would be okay.*

The language story

The first English word I learned was *jacaranda*. My English teacher
pointed to the jacaranda tree: "jaakkaaaraandaahhhhh." The
second word I learned was 'post office'. I didn't know what the
post office was, but I knew the building she pointed to was the
post office. I was seven years old. I could speak fluent Armenian,
Arabic and French. I could not speak English. My dad was fluent
in seven languages and my mum in four. A conversation in my
family would drift between the languages, sometimes in one
sentence. Australia brought forward a new challenge for us all,
one language: English.

Learning to speak in one language was challenging. I was
out of my depth. I was constantly making out the words and
figuring out what people were saying. Comprehension went
over my head. I was an English as a Second Language (ESL)
student, which meant I had a special teacher to sit with me for an
hour once a week to teach me English. In the first few months,
the teacher and I would walk out of the school grounds together
pointing to things. She would name them, and I would repeat.

To this day, I think in a blend of Armenian, Arabic, French,
and now English. I even structure my written sentences using
the grammatical principles of these different languages. I infuse
a blend of cultures in face-to-face conversations. I may seem
loud, in your face, over the top, crossing boundaries of personal
space – these are my cross-cultural ways of communicating.

These ways can be challenging for people who are unfamiliar with the robust conversing styles of Europe and the Middle East.

For many years, I thought my linguistic and cultural expressions were a barrier to connection with others. However, these experiences have taught me how to seek guidance when I need it. They have also taught me to listen to people in new ways, different ways, ways that serve my work and my clients as a chiropractor. Through these ways I learned to read the human body. As a result, I have developed my own ways of working that I am ready to pass on to others.

The shop story

My parents bought a food business in the small town of Forster. The hard part in a small coastal town initially were the insults and racial slurs. The gratification was satisfying when our little family-run business soared. Dad transformed the Aussie milk bar and burgers to a kebab palace. He did what he knew best and was out to introduce Middle Eastern food to a small fishing town. It was a success.

Another culture shock was how quiet and reserved the Australian culture was – I came from a loud and expressive culture that tended to speak with our hands and extraordinarily loud voices. One day a new employee raised an alarm to my mother, saying "You better get in quick, Raffi (my dad) and Therese are about to kill each other." My mother came racing in, only to discover another father and daughter expressive and passionate conversation. Everything was okay, and we all broke out into laughter. I'm sure it didn't help that we were all holding knives.

Shop time was family time. It was a family business. We showed our love through food and supporting the family business. We were all in and I spent my childhood being industrious.

This story reinforces my experience of being the outsider. Not only did I look different, I thought different, I talked different and I ate different. I share these stories because they are lifeworld experiences that strengthened me and equipped me for career adventures.

ᚤ

Natural law: Interconnectedness 1

You too have had experiences in your life that have shaped you into the powerful person you are today. I encourage you to identify perceived barriers you've overcome in your life and reflect on their impact, outcomes, and how they serve you now. Understanding how the challenges you've faced in life have strengthened you will make visible a range of tools and skills you already have available, as you embark on the journey towards your authentic clinical practice.

I invite you to take a moment to embrace your own foreignness, and identify the power it gives you by deepening your personal exploration with a list of explorative questions for identifying your 'transitional moments'. Give yourself the opportunity to step up, build momentum and take action steps with the exercises provided in Transitional Moments, below.

Transitional Moment
The Interconnectedness of Experiences of Your Younger Self

What lifeworld experiences have brought you to this point right now?

What events have stirred and shaken awake essential aspects inside you?

When have you felt like the hero and how did you navigate this triumph?

What was made solid inside you as a result of this experience?

When have you felt like the outsider and how did you navigate this experience?

What was strengthened inside you as a result of this experience?

What held you back?

What was strengthened in you as you overcame this challenge? You will have a story like my language story, something significant that held you back from moving forward to your own expression.

2

FINDING NEW GROUND

This chapter reflects on elements of the transitional journey practitioners may experience in making the leap from inspiration to an authentic practice. It includes a caution: beware the mimic trap. There is no point moving to your style of practice if you're going to mimic other practitioners. The joy in this journey is the transition to working authentically – your purpose, your clinic, your life, your way.

Inspiration

When I was 25 years old I made an appointment with a chiropractor. Why? Because I was curious. I had no idea what chiropractors did, and I wanted to find out. During that session, as I experienced my body releasing tension, I had three realisations:

1. I was responsible for my thoughts
2. I was responsible for my actions
3. I was responsible for my body.

In that moment it dawned on me that I was responsible for my life. *I had embodied the learning.* Inspired, I enrolled in a five-year university chiropractic degree. It was time to learn the wisdom of my body.

I was hungry for knowledge, and as a chiropractic student I

attended numerous talks by experienced chiropractors. I attended a talk by Dr Sue Brown, a chiropractor from Chicago who visited Australia in mid 2000s. Dr Brown introduced me to the interconnectedness of body-mind-spirit *and environment* through chiropractic principles. I resonated with her teachings, and she became my primary mentor.

Caught in a trap

As a fresh graduate with limited experience, I attended continuing education seminars. I felt limited in my skills and my authentic message. Ultimately, this magnified my self-doubt. I was continually comparing myself to peers who had been in practice for 20 years or more. The more I grew in myself, the more seminars I attended. Eventually it became clear that my peers might have more clinical experience than me, but at the seminar we were all at the same level: we were learning something new. I was no longer trapped by my own self-doubt. It vanished, to be replaced by an excited readiness to act. Because here's what else I learned: the experts had the same message. It was evident to me there was an observable process practitioners cycled through when stepping into their authentic practice, and it is these processes I am sharing with you in this book.

Y

Becoming your authentic self – the practitioner's journey

You, as a practitioner, walk a specific pathway in which you share your inherent authentic self-in-practice and message. Identifying, expressing and embodying your authentic practice message may, at times, seem hard and frustrating as you learn to trust yourself and your expression.

The pathway is not straight. It is cyclical in nature, inter-twining cycles with many twists and turns. I have mapped this and called it the 'the practitioner's journey'. It is a model you can use in a practical sense to assess, plan and action/execute your authentic practice journey. Setting time aside to reflect on this model periodically will assist you to observe, monitor and cele-brate your improvements and your evolution, from, for example, anxiety to authenticity and from self-doubt to confidence.

The self-doubt cycle is the first cyclic milestone. It involves coming to terms with your self-doubt, seeking help, having moments of unhappiness followed by letting go of attach-ments *because you have reached your threshold.* This letting go will transition you through invisible walls and barriers of life stag-nancy and hardship into sharing, refining and embodying your authentic message. At this point you will experience the benefits and joys of the second cyclic milestone: the self-belief cycle. The self-belief cycle is typically expressed as effortlessness and light. During this stage you will lead by example.

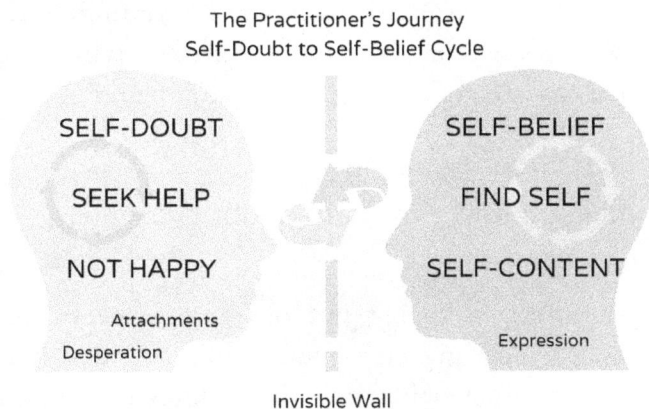

The Practitioner's Journey
Self-Doubt to Self-Belief Cycle

SELF-DOUBT		SELF-BELIEF
SEEK HELP		FIND SELF
NOT HAPPY		SELF-CONTENT
Attachments		Expression
Desperation		

Invisible Wall

Cyclic milestones
Cyclic milestone #1: the self–doubt cycle
The self-doubt cycle stages typically experienced by practitioners

11

on the journey towards expressing their authentic practice are as follows:

o Self-doubt
o Seeking help
o Not happy
o Crossing the invisible wall.

Cyclic milestone #2: the self-belief cycle

The self-belief cycle embodies empowerment and light. The stages practitioners will typically experience in this cycle are:

o Self-contentment
o Finding self
o Self-belief.

The key to successfully navigating these cyclic stages is knowing the difference between actions that take a small amount of time and actions that require more time and, therefore, greater effort. You cannot ignore the importance of these stages if you are to succeed in establishing your authentic practice. Practitioners who do not identify the various stages, actions or timings of actions, or confuse stages, actions and timings of actions, will experience entrapment in cycles of destruction and self-doubt.

The practitioner's journey

Cyclic milestone #1: The self-doubt cycle

Stage 1 – self-doubt

In the beginning, stepping out on your authentic practice journey will trigger gigantic amounts of self-doubt. It is new territory. You are stepping into the unknown. You will be navigating this territory during periods of extreme self-doubt. Self-doubt is sneaky. It has a way of getting into your mind and controlling your behaviour without you knowing. It will spark an avalanche of inner talk. This chatter is your inner critic, the ultimate ninja invader of your attention. It manifests as distractions, low concentration levels, impulsive twists, unnecessary reactions to situations, becoming over-emotional and lacking in routine structure. Self-doubt comes hand-in-hand with excuses and justifications, and these contribute to you delaying or rejecting ideas and actions that will inspire you.

It took me three years to pluck up my courage to leave contract jobs and work solely from my practice from home. Self-doubt ran havoc in my mind. I doubted I even had a clue about what I was doing. The truth was, deep down *I knew what I was doing*. Yet I was reinforcing my self-doubt through barrages of negative self-talk. I was seeking praise and approval from others – and when praise and approval were given, I was unable to hear, receive or comprehend what had been offered.

In treatment sessions I would start all confident and then before I could catch myself, I'd surrender my authenticity and revert back justifying to myself to my client. I was seeking approval. I was half-hearted about backing my authentic assessments.

Self-doubt comes in different forms for different people. Here's an example: in 2020 I was leading mentoring groups. I suggested to practitioners that a Facebook business page may be a good place to start letting people know they were in practice. Here is a list of responses I received, all of which are prime examples of self-doubt:

> "I don't like Facebook", "I don't know what to post", "I don't have a Facebook account", "I can't do that in my profession, it's illegal to have reviews", "I actually want to interact with people in person and not on social media", "Facebook is impersonal", "It's not going to reach anyone, it's pointless", "Do I really have to?"

Learning to identify and overcome self-doubt when it arises is essential to moving forward in your life and practice.

Think about what your self-doubt self-talk is likely to be. What excuses do you make for not acting upon ideas you know would move you forward in your life?

Stage 2 – seeking help

Overcoming self-doubt requires you to seek guidance, encouragement, support, help. Means for seeking help might include conversations with other practitioners, attending workshops to develop the personal skills and resources you need, and contracting people for particular tasks you don't have time to do, don't want to do or don't have the necessary skills to do. This aid will give you a huge sense of relief, and with relief will come momentum. This will stabilise you, reminding you you're on the right track. You will experience bouts of excitement and happiness and in the early stages they are unlikely to be long-lasting. Nonetheless, the act of seeking help and experiencing excitement about the path ahead are a pivotal shift from how you were feeling and *will* propel you forwards. You may get caught in the trap of chasing and seeking a momentary buzz of emotional release. Watch out for this trap.

For more than a decade I attended business, chiropractic and personal development seminars. It was great to connect with people, listen to speakers, give myself the space and time to plan. This was my avenue of seeking help. I began getting short-term gains from my action steps and this gave me the momentum I needed at that time. I learned to recognise some action steps needed shorter amounts of time to achieve, some action steps needed longer times to achieve, and some action steps were simple to achieve. Eventually, I understood that immaturity was getting in the way and hindering longer-term improvements. Nonetheless, seeking help enabled me to build momentum by actioning short-term gains and I can tell you, it was good to see the results.

Seeking help is a natural step on the path to authentic practice. It is the commencement of planting the seeds of transformation, and these seeds will need to be fertilised and nourished in order for them to flourish.

Think about how you might seek help.

Make a list of the actions you will take to seek help, and note why you have decided on that action.

Stage 3 – not happy

We are working with cycles. Chronic self-doubt is not a happy way to feel. Seeking help will help. And then, after a while, perhaps a week, two weeks, a month, you may return to being not happy. The core of your being still has the same issue regurgitating over and over. The momentum of the emotional release or buzz you experienced after seeking help has worn off and bouts of unhappiness kick in. This may lead you right back to your original self-doubt. And there we have it – the cycle begins again.

Through my seminars I actioned the quick steps and achieved the results, however the actions that required greater time to get results seemed out of reach. My momentum was deflated. Once again I was not happy.

Not happy is the point that you will think some version of the following: 'nothing works', 'this is not the profession you want', 'I should get a job', 'I have issues', and so on. I know these voices all too well, as I have walked this path with much rigor and intensity numerous times. It is at this point the authentic practitioner is likely to feel stuck in loops of self-doubt, seeking help and is not happy.

In 2013 I worked in a clinic which was a 90-minute drive in traffic from my house. After a 10-hour day, I would drive home and then spend another hour in the car unable to move, exhausted. I would park my car and cry. I was numb. I was not happy. Yes, I had clients; yes, I was making money; yes, I was practising – and there was a little bit of my soul I was destroying every single day. It was at this moment I evolved to my next phase. I decided to structure my practice and my message. I decided to work one-on-one with intensity, seeking help and counsel from individuals that I respected and trusted.

Thus I experienced the next evolutionary step in the practitioner's journey: letting go of attachments, in my case attachment to the 'job' with the 90-minute drive in traffic being 'the answer'.

> Watch out for moments when you are 'not happy'.
>
> What does not happy feel like for you?
>
> What signals does your body send in the early stages of not happy?
>
> If you can catch not happy early, you can take action to address the situation.
>
> What are you attached to that is creating the illusion of making you happy?
>
> What is the evolutionary step you can take now?

Stage 4 – the invisible wall

The invisible wall is not in the world, it is in your head. Crossing the invisible wall marks the transition from letting go of old attachments to allowing your new world to become visible through your actions.

Letting go of attachments is easier said than done. Perhaps you, too, have experienced lying on the floor crying your eyes out, secluding yourself, feeling numb, consuming substances such as excessive alcohol, cigarettes, weed and sugar – all of which perpetuate self-doubt and unhappiness, and are chronic generators of self-disappointment. The reality is, if you really do want what you say you want – your authentic self in authentic practice – you have to surrender habitual behaviours that undermine your efforts and surrender *all* your attachments, including attachments to how things are supposed to go and how things are supposed to look in order for your authentic way to emerge. This is the hard bit and it is integral to the process.

The experience of letting go can feel difficult, hard, undoable, not possible. Most of us are unaware of the underlying attachments we need to let go in order to move forward. With hindsight, your attachment will be in-your-face obvious. Here's an example: in 2018 I set up a beta group to trial my new coaching program. I proposed standardising prices for treatment, thereby eliminating children's and pensioner pricing. The backlash from this simple suggestion was eye opening:

"The poor pensioners that are sick", "How can you charge them full price when they need care?", "It's too much on the families, they won't be able to come when they need to", "How can you do that? It's not ethical", "There is no way of abolishing discounts", "That is greedy".

With hindsight, I realise the baseline of my attachment to special pricing was defensive as I did not understand why discount pricing was employed in clinics for providing the same allocated time and service. Wanting to do good is a foundational value in my authentic practice, however I have discovered there are more successful ways of doing good for the community that are authentic for me than discounts for treatments. I found the special pricing for pensioners and children created one-sided financial benefits that came at the expense of my time and income. I was allocating the same time, if not more for a discount rate, this created an inner annoyance in myself.

To let go of an attachment you must first recognise the

attachment. Attachments manifest in many forms. I've listed four for your consideration and exploration: thought, action, physical and emotional attachments.

Thought attachments

Thought attachments are internalised expressions of your destructive inner-critic ninja run riot. Examples for the practitioner seeking authentic practice include: success is out of reach, I will never make the money, I'm not making money, I do not have the skills, I am a failure, I am the outsider, people are not responding to me, other people are doing better than me, I am a late starter, no-one is listening, what I'm doing is wrong, I'm an emotional mess, I fear missing out, rich people are evil and avoid taxes, other people get away with things.

Action attachments

Action attachments that inhibit the practitioner seeking authentic practice include: refusing to structure your time, scrolling aimlessly on social media, engaging in gossip, being continually distracted, conversing in pointless exchanges, resisting tasks you know you have to do – admin, tax, cooking, cleaning.

Physical attachments

The primary physical attachment that inhibits the practitioner seeking authentic practice is perpetual physical exhaustion. Common symptoms and outcomes of *attachment to* physical exhaustion are dizziness, weight gain, menstrual pain, back pain, busy-ness with no progression, dullness with lack of excitement, general low mood, possible depression, low clinic numbers, no client bookings.

Why would I be attached to physical exhaustion, I hear you ask? If you are not taking action to head off physical exhaustion then you are *attached* to the exhaustion. The likely reason for this will be you are hiding. Perhaps you are fearful about what's up ahead in your journey? Perhaps you fear further exposure and risk on your path to authentic practice? Perhaps you feel the journey is asking too much?

Keep going. You've got this.

Emotional attachments

Examples of emotional attachments that inhibit the practitioner seeking authentic practice are: holding on to friendships that no longer serve the evolution of you, holding on to clients that no longer serve the evolution of your practice.

The self-doubt cycle is like chasing your tail. You seek out quick fixes and get-rich-quick schemes. You feel stuck. And then comes the point where you have had enough of the cycle. You are no longer interested in engaging with your inner turmoil. You're bored with the cycle. In order for you to move forward in authentic practice, it is imperative that you identify and take action to address your attachments.

What are your attachments?

They might be small, they might be huge.

List your thought attachments.

List your action attachments.

List your physical attachments.

List your emotional attachments.

What action do you need to take to overcome each attachment?

What actions do you take to 'do good' in your community that in reality do align with your authentic practice?

Desperation/expression

In order for the new world of authentic practice to become visible to you, you must cross what I call 'the invisible wall'. Firstly, however, it's important to become familiar with two distinct states from which you may be operating your business: desperation and expression.

Desperation

Operating your practice from desperation is a lot like repeatedly hitting your head against the invisible wall and wanting it not to hurt. Trust me, I know. The operational mode of desperation is the desperate wanting of something to save you: the new car, the money, the clinic, the relationship and, no matter what you do, it doesn't come. You work hard, really hard, you think you are getting somewhere, and then, boom, you are back to square one. In this state, you do not feel safe. You feel exposed. You are confused. You lose track of time. You plan poorly. You feel desperation *a lot* of the time.

Expression

Operating your practice from expression is a joy. In expression, you *know* your task is to express *you* in all parts of your life and practice. This is your authentic self in practice. Practise methodically, diligently, authentically and your outcomes will improve accordingly.

Desperation and expression are different sides of the same coin. Here are two experiences from my own life where I transformed desperation into expression.

Desperation

At university I was a study nerd. I was desperate to pass and worked hard to study with my learning difficulties. This hard work ethic made me an intense personality and scared many

20

people and friendships away. Consequently, I was desperate to succeed.

My desperation was failing to express an ounce of what I needed and wanted in many areas of my life. My studies were the priority. My expectations were unrealistic, my life was way out of balance, my stress load was toxic. I started falling apart. I needed to reassess my ways of behaviour and attitude.

Expression

I reassessed the prioritising of my studies. I needed to form friendships again.

I decided every Friday night I would go out to a bar and socialise. Going out was the key to my success and my studies. Paradoxically, by no longer making study the core existence of my life my studies improved. I let go of my attachments, and with that came great nights of laughter, fun, friendships, food, music and dancing. I sailed through my studies with great results. It took me four years of self-inflicting stress to learn this lesson.

Desperation

In 2012 I made two decisions:

1. I would undertake an intense neurological-based seminar series of eight modules, and
2. To save my pennies for the program, I would no longer buy clothing unless I had worn every piece of clothing in my cupboard at least once. However inadvertently, I was punishing myself.

Expression

During the second module of the intense seminar series, I needed to clear my head. I decided to go out and do some window shopping in my lunch break. I ended up breaking my no new clothes rule and bought three pairs of tights at $10 each. The purchase of tights brought me so much joy, I remember the moment to this day. It was a landmark occasion for me as I let go of suppression of my desire and acted on my expression. What's more, I did not complete the eight modules. I stopped after the second module and was very happy that I did. And in case you're wondering, I loved those tights and wore them well into their demise.

As simple as these two examples of desperation/expression may appear, they were challenging in real time. I experienced stress and the collapse of important friendships as I constantly banged my head on the invisible wall. Once I crossed the invisible wall, however, my authentic expression was launched.

In the end, crossing the invisible wall was easy. It was the resistance to it that was hard.

Reflect on moments in your own life when you have crossed the invisible wall from desperation to expression.

When were you acting from desperation?

How did you express your desperation?

What were the outcomes you experienced when you were acting from desperation?

What action did you take to transform desperation to expression?

How are you better off for having surrendered your desperation for authentic expression?

Ϋ

The practitioner's journey
Cyclic milestone #2: The self-belief cycle
Stage 5 – self-contentment

Once you have crossed the invisible wall, you will experience the joy of self-contentment. From here there is a natural progression to increasing capabilities for discerning what to share, when and with whom. Self-contentment is your first big step to knowing who you are in authentic practice. In this stage you will simplify what you do and you will become comfortable with your audience. Self-contentment is a peace of knowing. The peace of knowing has many expressions:

o the peace you have made with yourself
o the peace you have made with your practice
o the peace you have made with the service you provide
o the peace you have made with the profession
o the peace you have made with who you wish to interact with.

As a result, you are able to identify the benefits of your practice to your clients and feel confident in your contribution to people in your community. You are no longer controlled by previously perceived higher powers and external forces. You stride with pride into your authentic self. You 'get it' and you 'find yourself'. You see the bigger picture, you understand your *why* and you share your *why* with the world.

Stage 6 – finding self
Finding self is the big picture. It is understanding, it is acceptance. You are in harmony with yourself. When you live with understanding, acceptance and harmony you can be confident you are living in alignment yourself. Life is easy. Magic is everywhere, even in the smallest of interactions. This is the other side of the invisible wall. You are no longer constantly seeking help and reassurance from others – you have found this in yourself.

Stage 7 – self-belief
When you step into self-belief you exude your authentic self and your authentic practice. You embody your contribution,

you know the role you play, and you know the mark you make is sizeable. You know you do not have to be famous or have thousands of followers on social apps. You simply know your space in the world, and you are on the journey to the next evolution of you.

The following diagram depicts the cyclic milestones. You will notice that the journey from self-doubt to self-belief is a mirror image: from seeking help to finding self, from not happy to self-contentment. The dotted line in the middle is represents the invisible wall.

Natural law: Interconnectedness 2

As you know, the practitioner's journey has its cycles. As you step into your own practice, you may cycle from self-doubt to self-belief or you may experience a dominant cycle that takes a long time to recognise. I encourage you to reflect on your authentic practice cycle and identify the invisible walls that you have encountered or may encounter.

Transitional Moment
Your Practitioner Journey

Which stage of your practitioner journey do you identify with in this moment in time?

The journey may seem linear; however, it is cyclical in nature.

Are you more dominant in the self-doubt cycle or the self-belief cycle?

What is the nature of the invisible wall you need to cross?

Identify moments in your life, outside of work and practice; when have you transitioned from self-doubt to self-belief?

How did this transition impact your life?

3

MAPPING NEW TERRITORY

Stepping up into your own practice is just like preparing for a journey through new territory. You need a map. You need discipline. You need fresh practice delivery methods to guide you. Importantly, you need new focus to avoid distractions such as mind chatter, negative self-talk, comparing yourself to others, and other negative forces that can consume the unprepared and easily distracted (which is most of us when we're anticipating or immersed in unknown territory).

Don't get held back because you don't know. Now is not the time for those patterns – conscious and otherwise – to take charge of your practitioner's journey to authentic practice.

This final chapter of *Part 1: Stepping Up* introduces The 3Ds: Discernment, Discipline, Delivery. This process of exploring The 3Ds is equivalent to assessing, planning and actioning. The 3Ds are a cyclic practice: Discerning discusses vital practices and processes you can develop, to maximise the benefits of Discipline and the satisfaction of authentic practice Delivery, whilst exhilarating in the ally-ship of connection, peace, freedom, joy, power, and magic.

Y

The 3Ds

The First D: Discernment

How are distractions limiting you?

In running your practice, the following behaviours are likely to surface: concealed victimhood, avoidance, stagnation, rumination and overwhelm, saviour complex and exhaustion. If you're fortunate, you will be aware of them. If you're not aware of them, it is essential they be addressed early if you are to experience the magic of successful authentic practice.

Paradoxically, these same behaviours may have been the impetus for you stepping up into your authentic practice in the first place – so that you can subconsciously work on them. *Yeah, I know, right? Healer, heal thyself.*

First distraction: concealed victimhood

Regardless of the endeavour you've embarked upon, when you step into new territory various behaviours and/or reactions will surface as you venture into the unknown. You may 1. not be aware of these behaviours, 2. be very well aware of them, and/or 3. you may already be actively working on shifting them.

Running the same negative story in your mind results in habitual behavioural patterns that do not serve you. It is essential that you transform habitual negative stories and behaviours into progressive action. If you do not you are vulnerable to becoming a victim of your own behaviour. Yes, you can be your own victim.

A great example of concealed victimhood is blame. Blame is concealing the fact you think you have no control over or power in a situation. Though unconscious, blame can be detected in language and thought patterns. Conversations that conclude with blaming parents and parenting styles, the medical system, the government, your partner's behaviours or your culture are examples of concealed victimhood.

If you do not pay attention to such expressions of victimhood, you run the risk of concealing the problem. This will perpetuate the behaviour and undermine your authenticity. It takes courage to recognise that you are victimising yourself. It takes even greater courage to act heroically on your own behalf.

A personal example: it took me months to introduce myself to the chiropractor down the end of the same street as me. Why? Because I thought he would be upset that I decided to open up on the same street. I had an idea in my head that he had greater authority because he was here before me. My repetitive underlying thought was: 'I should not be here. This is not my territory.' I perpetuated my behaviour by anchoring feelings of anxiety and nervousness in my body every time I drove by his clinic, every time I looked him up online, every time I needed to walk down the road – so I'd take the longer route to avoid walking past the front of his clinic. Eventually I mustered my allies. I walked down the street and introduced myself sheepishly, with an unnecessarily high voice I might add, and found out he was a lovely human. Instantly I relaxed and I invited him to my practice for monthly practice sessions.

Stop running. Reveal yourself to yourself and others.

Second distraction: avoidance

It is a fact of being human that we run from what we fear. When we run from our internal fears, those fears will run us down and they will keep running us down until we have the courage to face them.

An example of avoidance might be the habit of avoiding conversations that feel like confrontations. Avoidance can also manifest as frustration about a lack of progression in your practice, particularly due to comparing yourself to others. This might be comparing your skills, your network of relationships, your income. Unaddressed, avoidance will manifest in your life in general. Comparing your progress to others' will cause you to withdraw, to hide.

If you do not face your internal fears, you will get more of what you do not want. This is natural law. You must stop. Hold your ground. And tell yourself the truth about what it is you fear.

A personal example: in 2011 I was miserable in someone else's clinical practice. I thought moving to another clinic would be the answer. In 2012 I took on an extra clinic job, once a day in a new location. Even though this brought in additional money, I was still miserable. In 2013 I moved to another new clinic. This time I was even more miserable. *My heart was not in it.*

I had told myself a change in scenery, new people and increased income would get me out of my misery. I was wrong. My main avoidance was stepping up to opening my own clinic and providing my authentic service in my authentic way.

I created many excuses and justifications as to why I should not, could not open my own practice. Rather than stepping up, I was bitching and complaining about everyone else and their practices. I avoided the real issue: my internal dialogue of self-judgment because I was 'different' and had an 'original message' I needed to share. My avoidance was holding up my self-progression, in life and clinical practice. This, in turn, was robbing me of the possibilities I could otherwise be creating, all the while telling myself my time would come.

Stop avoiding. Start facing.

Third distraction: stagnation

Stagnation refers to lack of progress on your journey, specifically in the context of comparing yourself with other practitioners.

This is a debilitating dynamic, and a primary reason why you must face the first and second distractions listed above: concealed victimhood and avoidance.

A personal example: in 2001 I was studying a business degree at Newcastle University. The statistics lecturer liked to share messages of aspiration post-graduation. These were focused around one theme: aim high. For example, upon graduating we were supposed to aim high by earning $60,000 in our first year out as a graduate. I was a young, impressionable undergrad; $60,000 was big money and I fixated that number in my head.

Fast forward to my first-year tax return as a practitioner when I earned a relatively pitiful $30,000. I concluded that I had not made it. I had not progressed. My life was a failure.

With hindsight, comparing myself to that lecturer's flippant aspiration was foolish. That aspiration had no relevance to me or my world. I had denied myself the truth, which was that I had completed five years of study and was a new entry into the chiropractic field in a city with a saturated market. First and foremost, I was figuring out how to be a clinician. The subconscious $60,000 success/failure bar had been like shrapnel in my brain. It was concealed from me. When it surfaced, it resulted in a period of disheartenment and internal stagnation – until I faced the reality that feeding my woes would not contribute to my progression. Rather than re-enforcing my lack, awareness of this subtle shrapnel became the impetus for kicking into gear the discipline and delivery I needed to achieve the income that would eventually become my authentic reality.

Fourth distraction: rumination and overwhelm

There is a vast difference between self-reflection and rumination. The first is a tool for progressing your understanding of circumstances and events in your work and your life. The second, rumination, is a spiral of navel gazing that will immobilise your efforts and destroy your spirits. Self-reflection leads to inspired action, on your own behalf and on behalf of others. Rumination will lead to debilitating feelings of being overwhelmed and an inability to cope.

A personal example: in 2014, I witnessed the following scenario. A new mother was referred to Practitioner A, with whom I worked. She attended the chiropractic clinic for the first time, baby in tow. The baby was crying, the mother doing her best to soothe it. Alas, crying is what babies do. Practitioner B barged into the room and, without consent, picked up the baby and said the baby was crying due to cranial issues, that the baby needed treatment, and they had the qualifications for this treatment. Practitioner A was gobsmacked. She asked Practitioner B to leave the treating room, and the baby. The client was shocked, really annoyed, and, justifiably, walked out of the clinic with her baby.

This scene was real, and it happened to me. I am Practitioner A. This incident still leaves me lost for words. Had I ruminated on the event, I would have churned up a bitter, never-ending story about how I should have done this and should have done that, which in reality would have served as a prime example of both the dangers of rumination and concealed victimhood. By turning to self-reflective practice, however, I discovered that it was not me who lacked clinical boundaries – it was my colleague. By reflecting on this experience I was also able to assess my responsibilities and responses to the situation. I was positioned to stabilise and solidify my own boundaries, ensuring that such an event could not occur in my clinical practice again.

Collisions with people in our lives are inevitable. Such events can cause us to ruminate and feel overwhelmed. Or you can use such events as an opportunity to know your boundaries and reinforce them accordingly.

Rumination is a distraction that will inhibit your authentic practice success.

Fifth distraction: saviour complex

Healing practitioners tend to share the trait of being natural care-givers. When you run your own practice, beyond the reach of corporate clinical targets and practices, your care-giver style is going to quickly surface. When it does, you may find your care-giver style collides with or overrides your business systems and principles.

The saviour complex might be defined as giving too much of yourself away – literally. There is a difference between 'saving' your clients and your healthy expression of your natural care-giving practices. When your saviour complex undermines your business *values* (not necessarily just your bottom line), you can be sure you are out of alignment with your care-giving.

A personal example: in 2014 I organised my first chiropractic mission trip to Armenia. I was joined by three other chiropractors. We visited remote communities, orphanages and rehabilitation centres, sharing the chiropractic message and adjusting locals who needed care. In 2016, I was contacted to be partially sponsored by a group who wanted me to return to Armenia. In exchange, I received accommodation, and they organised the communities I would visit and translators. I accepted and took three chiropractors with me. Unbeknownst to me, in return for this 'sponsorship' we were to service more than seven hundred people a day in different locations. On day three of the five-day trip, I requested a day off. We were worked to the bone. I told the organiser that my people were tired and that we needed a break. The organisers refused my request, and a heated discussion ensued. One of my practitioners whispered to me: "Let's just go and do it to shut them up." I looked this practitioner straight in the eye and said: "No".

We were exhausted. We were practitioners, not machines. We would rest.

This situation highlighted the potentially devastating outcomes of the saviour complex. When you give more than you are able, when you do not set the terms of your engagement, people will take as much licence as you give them. The belief that we must constantly deliver because someone else says we should is insane.

As a result of this experience I made a vow: if I am to place my hands on anyone, I will charge for my service. I will not exchange, nor will I gift. This philosophy has served me well. It has ensured I understood the value of my work. It has taught me how to set the conditions and parameters of how and when and with whom I will work. It has eliminated my need to 'save' anyone.

Your skills and time and personal resources are worth more than their weight in gold. If you are in existence, and you are, then there is a reason why you are here and a message that you are here to share. This is your purpose in life and it does no-one any good if you are unable to sustain yourself as you go about sharing your message.

Many practitioners struggle with this, even those long-experienced with clinical practice. There comes a time when you need to grow up and be grown up. Accept the value you have placed on your skills and increase your prices if there is an inner call to do so. Learn to charge without justification.

You have worth. People will come.

Beware the saviour complex: it can fool you into thinking you are doing good, and there *will* be a price to pay – for you, your business, and your clients.

Sixth distraction: exhaustion

I have spoken to chiropractors, surgeons, dentists, masseuses, psychotherapists, homeopaths, and more – and regardless of their practice modality, they are commonly prone to exhaustion. Exhaustion among practitioners is rampant. It is ubiquitous across healing modalities for a reason that is inherent to our work: empathic clinical listening. Empathic listening without rest is no longer empathy. Empathy without rest will ensure you are not treating your client to the best of your ability. We owe our clients and ourselves the best care-giving practices we have to offer. We cannot do this if we are exhausted. Exhaustion is a fast-track to burnout. Sure-fire signs you are on the road to burnout are perpetual exhaustion, resulting in loss of interest in your work. Eventually, burnout can drive practitioners out of practice.

I have experienced my share of exhaustion in clinical practice. Here is my burnout prevention strategy: the joy period. The joy period is limited to four hours' straight, during which time I provide care for as many people as I like. I have learned that, after four hours, I lose my joy for practice. I begin to resent what I am doing and the people who come to me for care, which is not fair on either my clients or myself. After four hours I need to rest.

Discovering the joy period was a 'eureka' moment. My daily mood and overall mental health no longer suffered from over-work. More than four hours' straight destabilised my wellbeing. Unhappiness would come over me and, when unaddressed, this always resulted in exhaustion.

This doesn't *necessarily* mean I only work in the clinic four hours a day. It means I have learned when to rest and when to work, in cycles that are sustainable for my own health.

Empathic listening is not just hearing your clients' stories. As you and your client step into the space of healing all sorts of information and energies begin interacting and interrelating between you. As the process of releasing and healing is taking place, the practitioner's body is doing a different kind of listening. It is likely she or he will absorb fragments of the releasing information and energy. The practitioner who is not skilled at moving these energies on will become exhausted, weighed down by the releasing energies infiltrating the room. There is an art to observing, witnessing, allowing these energies to move on without absorbing them ourselves. *I am yet to get there.*

It is unwise for the clinical practitioner to blame the client for this dynamic. This will only cause you to resent your clients as you pass thoughtless judgement on 'their crap'. Their crap is why they have come to see you. You are the healing practitioner. It is your responsibility to ensure exhaustion and burnout prevention strategies to protect your own health and wellbeing.

Whatever you are struggling with in clinical practice, whether it's your overbearing workload or the energetic releases of your clients, your health and wellbeing is paramount. If you cannot recover your energy and your joy fully every single day, wind back – and watch the benefits of increasing joy roll in to your clinic and your life.

Discernment

Discernment is your capacity for overcoming distractions. To discern is to choose, consciously decide: Is this behaviour right for me in this moment? Discernment is your superpower for overcoming distractions.

Intuition versus instinct

Early in my career I would hear practitioners use terms such as 'gut feel' or 'feeling things'. My understanding at that time was that those who were able to 'feel things' had intuition. Maturing in my skills, I became curious about the distinctions between emotional reactions and intuition.

In 2017, I attended a training where the premise taught was

'intuition does not exist'. Many students gasped with horror at the idea and rebutted the notion. I was rather intrigued, because in my experience the teacher and her teachings demonstrated significant amounts of intuition. The concept of 'intuition does not exist' did not trigger a response from me.

I decided to explore the notion that 'intuition does not exist'. I'm pleased I did, as I now have an entirely new appreciation of the concept. Intuition is not a special power. It is not a thing that is separate from you or outside of you. It is you wanting to figure out your inner way of interpreting, analysing and solving a situation. However, if you do not have a method for analysing or verbalising your findings, you may fall back on 'intuition' to avoid interpreting and understanding the steps, the logic and the intricacies of your practice. Leaning too quickly into 'intuition' dismisses information you may otherwise glean from the wisdom of your inner listening. You may start to second guess yourself. Intuition does not require conscious reasoning. It can been seen as fluffy, even though the answer may be right if there is no logical reasoning.

Instinct, on the other hand, is a primal inborn response that is hardwired into your body. Instinct has fixed patterns that respond to stimuli. For example, the mating rituals of birds or the way pregnant whales can pause pregnancy for up to a year if the environment is unsafe (an embryonic diapaus). Examples of instinct in humans include babies' reflexes or adrenalin responses of defence when being attacked. These are instincts and there is no second-guessing yourself.

Logic and reasoning are your secret sauces behind your practice. They are your ways of listening and understanding your methods and practices. They are your internal signature structure and they are vital to harmonising yourself with your practice.

Your premonitions, gut feelings, and bodily responses are real. Your internal intelligence and your body's wisdom are asking deeper listening from you.

I invite you to reflect on the distinction between intuition and instinct.

What is intuition? And describe how it may be experienced through bodily sensations.

What is instinct? And describe how it may be experienced through bodily sensations.

Describe the structure of your internal signature that you bring to your practice.

Keep returning to this exercise to evolve your understanding of your authentic practice.

Natural law: Interconnectedness 3

Stepping up into your authentic practice will level up all of who you know yourself to be in the world. You will overcome concealed victimhood and learn to face that which you avoid. You will conquer stagnation. You will prevail over the risk of rumination. You will shed your saviour complex once and for all. You are no longer seeking the approval of others, you are beyond the potential for exhaustion. The First D: Discernment is your starting place for ensuring every day is a joy-full day.

Transitional Moment
The Interconnectedness of Distractions: A Personal Exploration

How do you express victimhood in your personal or practice life?

Where are you stagnating in your personal or practice life?

> List the situations that are likely to make you feel overwhelmed in your personal or practice life.
>
> When have you played the saviour in your personal or practice life?
>
> How do you know when you are heading for physical exhaustion – what are its symptoms?

Keys to Authentic Success

Keys to authentic success: commitment, support, expression, expansion, awareness

When I began the intensive mastery program with my mentor, Dr Sue Brown, I needed to ensure I could participate in such a rigorous program *and* maintain balance in other areas of my life. I wanted to be sure I could complete the program with joy, and that life's pendulum would not swing in extremes.

The key was commitment. The commitment to the program was a no-brainer. It was easy to make that commitment, as I knew the direction I wanted to head in with my practice. I was committed to the program, which meant I was committed to the significant travel and expenses involved.

The support I needed to sustain balance came through my family, my travel agent and other mastery program participants. None of these people questioned or made comments about my choices – that is not support. They knew I was after something, and they wished me well on each and every trip. My flight itinerary was Sydney-Los Angeles-Chicago return. Sometimes I would make stops in Los Angeles to visit my uncle for the day. My uncle's excitement about my semi regular visits was encouraging, and my parents enjoyed the fact that I had a contact in the US. The constant communication brought our widespread family closer together. My travel agent understood my flight needs, and having someone to be able to contact with questions and book flights that suited me meant someone had my back. By choosing a small travel agency I was able to develop a longstanding, supportive relationship.

During the program my expression was ever-evolving. I was expressing an increase in confidence in my hands-on skills and clinical findings. I was expressing my desires for holidays and adventures that in the past I would have believed were out of reach. The expansion of my consciousness was tenfold during the program – another form of expression. I grew to see myself as someone expansive. I *became* expansive. I could no longer stay small, and my life-awareness increased. This complete surrender to my authentic journey, and the mustering of a network to support and sustain me, awakened the capacity to view the bigger picture in events I may previously have thought of as catastrophic.

The Keys to Authentic Success embody five elements: commitment, support, expression, expansion and awareness.

1. **Commitment: to yourself and your clients**
   This commitment is the acknowledgement and acceptance that there will be pleasure with pain, fear with faith, and reward with retribution.
   Your commitment to your practice and your goals is a mindset.
   Cultivate your mindset.
2. **Support**
   Your mindset needs support. This support requires like-minded people to support your journey. These people might be individuals, groups, friends and/or family – people you are confident share your values, and with whom you can talk things through vulnerably, without feeling judged.
3. **Expression**
   It can be challenging expressing yourself in the world as yourself. However sharing your expression – not hiding it,

or being shy about your message, or nervous about how you want your message to come across – is vital to this journey. You will experience times when you are caught up with 'what other people will think'. The antidote is simple: act for your authentic self.

If not now, when?

4. Expansion

Be ready to expand your mind and your capacity for faith. Being cynical is your enemy on this journey. So, too, self-criticism. These are unnecessary burdens you do not need to carry. Lay them down and watch with wonder as you expand, with your expression of your authentic message.

5. Awareness

Utilise your capacity for opening your awareness. You will do this by quietening your mind. Techniques for quietening include meditation, exercise, hiking, camping, being in nature, fasting, good sleep, being present in conversation, and *asking questions*. Asking questions will expand your awareness. Everyone who crosses your path is a potential messenger for you. When you have an opportunity to speak to people, be curious, open your awareness, ask questions.

Read through the five keys to successful authentic practice listed above and reflect on the following:

Commitment: are you genuinely committed to your authentic self in authentic practice? Reflect on what this means to you. Reflect on where you feel your commitment is lacking and make a list of actions you can realistically take to step into your authenticity. If not now, when?

Support: what support networks do you need to put in place now to sustain you on your journey? What steps do you need to establish these networks?

Expression: describe your desired self-expression. Are you living this expression?

Expansion: what toxic elements are getting in the way of your authenticity? Are you cynical? Are you self-critical? What steps will you take to clear your energy field to make way for your full expression in the world?

Awareness: what steps are you taking each and every day towards quietening your mind?

AWARENESS

EXPANSION

COMMITMENT

KEYS TO
SUCCESS

EXPRESSION

SUPPORT

Part 2: STEPPING OUT

NATURAL LAW
CORRESPONDENCE

4

FUELLING YOUR FIRE: OWNING YOUR GENIUS

Welcome to the next phase of your journey towards authentic practice. As you begin *Part 2: Stepping Out* you may feel immersed in brain fog as you seesaw between replaying thoughts of the past and thinking about the future, only to bypass the present. The answer may lie in lifting the veil that is masking your true reality and your true existence. To ensure your success we need to disconnect you from your day-to-day fog. How? By striking a POSE. Much like daily practices such as meditation, yoga or ritual, embedding POSE into the fabric of your being will eliminate cyclic and distressing brain fog and elevate you to the life you long to be living.

๛

Strike that POSE: a 4–step model for practical use

Pattern, Own, Shift, Emancipate.

1. identify your *Pattern*
2. acknowledge your pattern by *Owning* it
3. prepare for a *Shift* in your perspective
4. stand by to *Emancipate* yourself from limitations that have cobbled, or will cobble, your authenticity and your practice.

Are you ready? Going about your authentically messaged practice on a daily basis is to bind these steps into one unit. It's time to strike that POSE.

Pattern

There is a pattern you are wanting to shift. Identifying your pattern may be easy, it may be challenging. Identify your pattern.

Own

Owning your pattern is you choosing to accept the call to transformation. Owning it is accepting you want to do things differently. Accepting the call is understanding you have done nothing wrong. You are not doing life wrong; however, you do need to start owning every aspect of your life.

Shift

Once you have taken ownership, there is a shift in the air. To sustain your momentum, you may choose a mentor to study under or choose a method to emancipate yourself from what has been holding you back.

Emancipate

The inner peace that comes with release from your past turmoil.

Moving forward with POSE

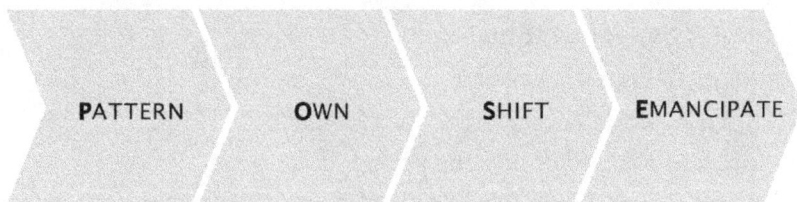

PATTERN   OWN   SHIFT   EMANCIPATE

Over more than ten years I have witnessed a common pattern

amongst international practitioners. When I've had the opportunity to speak to them, I've asked a specific question: "Why do you do what you do?"

Their immediate response is always a breath-hold, followed by a stare or a glazed gaze. Then comes their response: "I don't know."

I continue: "That's okay, make something up."

This comment tends to be a trigger. Replies are often defensive, loaded with justification and occasionally anger. Yet it is important to me to ask this question – if an expert in a field doesn't know why they do what they do, then that's a red alert for me. *What are you doing guiding others if you don't know why you are doing so?*

In 2019 I ran a workshop for practitioners in Barcelona. It was the most memorable workshop I ever ran. When I asked participants 'Why do you do what you do?', one participant replied: "I'm not doing this exercise. I am not going to make something up, because if I don't mean it and I have verbalised it, then that resonance will carry through my practice."

I replied: "You are welcome to change it at any time. It is not set in stone."

She replied: "If you say it, yes it is."

This woman was frightened of being wrong and she was frightened of being visible to others: *I am not enough.* This was her pattern. Now, if you share this woman's concern that you don't want to say something in case the resonance carries through, how many times have you said: "I am going to win the lottery?" Has that resonance carried through?

What is the pattern that is undermining your authentic practice? Can you accept that it is okay to be creative, to let your imagination speak for you for a while? Can you allow yourself to make something up? You can't get it wrong. You are hardly likely to create a negative answer. Fear will hold you back and limit you.

Answering this question will move you forward. Besides, your insight into why you do what you do should grow and evolve with you, as you grow and evolve in authentic practice.

It took me three months for me to articulate my own 'why I do what I do'. I was coached through it, and consequently developed POSE as a method for speeding up the process for tasks that I needed to be coached through.

Prior to finding my 'why', if you asked me why I do what I do I would have been silent and numb. My pattern was to freeze. I owned this pattern by first identifying my silent and frozen behaviour when I was put on the spot. Once I understood that I would freeze, I would blurt out the first thing that would come to mind, and of course most of the time the words and sentences did not make sense. Once I became more skilled at owning what-ever came out of my mouth, a shift happened. I began to form articulate sentences. And voilà, along came a sense of freedom. In this way I started helping others formulate their why.

This entire experience was expressive, expansive, awakening and highly emancipating.

Here is my current response to why I do what I do: I do what I do so that you can uplift your life and live life in a way that you did not think was possible.

POSE EXERCISES

To begin sharing your WHY with your clients, start by asking yourself, "Why do I do what I do?"

Work it out, find an answer, write it down.

Evolve your answer.

Check in with yourself regularly: Why do you do what you do?

Your pattern is what others see in you. You, however, may be blind to your patterns.

A brave way of finding your patterns is to enquire of your friends: "What patterns do you see in me that hold me back?

What are your patterns? List them.

Are you willing to own your patterns? Why do you want to blame others for why you do what you do? Monitor these experiences.

Find your patterns, own your patterns, shift your patterns and experience emancipation.

Now, strike your POSE with confidence and clarity.
You know who you are.

Natural law: Correspondence 4

Congratulations on making significant progress towards authentic practice. It's time now explore how the various elements introduced so far correspond to each other. These elements are:

o   the first of The 3Ds: Discernment
o   the keys to authentic awareness: commitment, support, expression, expansion and awareness
o   POSE.

Identifying the patterns that hinder you from moving forward to the next stage is vital to your capacity for living and working authentically. Being skilled in these processes will enable you to intercept new patterns before they intercept you.

Transitional Moment
Corresponding to Life's Pattern

Return to the first of The 3Ds: Discernment. How is each stage relevant to you at this point in your journey?

Revisit the Keys to Authentic Success. Explore how each key can help you move beyond the distractions limiting you and holding you back.

Now let's run them through POSE.

What patterns underpin your distractions?

How will you own the patterns that underpin your distractions?

What action will you take to shift the patterns that underpin your distractions?

Describe the feeling of emancipation - and remember this.

Why have you chosen healthcare as your profession?

A word on courage

As you embark on your transition to your running your own practice, you will likely experience sustained periods of feeling alone. I'll be honest with you, it can be a long and lonely journey. You may at times feel as if you are the only human in your sphere who is brave enough to stand for her truth and share her authentic message with the world. You are walking your reality, which you trust 100%. And yet this reality may hurl you into the fires of transformation and the washpools of change. All brave action demands we navigate the unknown. During my own time of transition I recall experiencing visions, colours, sounds and tastes that were not witnessed by anyone at all other than me. I felt if I shared my experiences I would sound crazy. I found courage. I held my ground. I walked my path. I trusted the reality that was growing deep within me. I claimed my authentic message. This is what it is to step out on your own path.

This is what transformation asks from us.

You may not see colours. You will however be cooked in the cauldron of change. To resist your summons to take this journey is to stay right where you are — and that is fine, if right where you are is enough for you. For me, transformation was the only path. Once I accepted the realities of the journey, I learned to find it natural to walk solo.

That said, once I looked — and I mean looked long and hard into the cauldron of change, I understood that I had never been alone on this journey. All the way through I was held and guided. There was no other way to the transformation I sought, other than the way I was led. I learned to accept all of what was and is in my environment, including the ideologies of others who would project their fears and uncertainties and belief systems onto me. I remained true to my path and learned to protect myself and my sphere of influence.

If you can find strength enough to hold your courage as you enter the realms of transformation, you, too, will discover that you are held and guided through the processes of change as you navigate your path to your own genius. Regardless of the ideologies that dominate the broader environment in which you live, as you walk your path in your own practice you will find calm and peace. This peace was given to you as your birthright. It is peace that is unimaginably tender as you preserve the perfection of your life and your path.

It is the peace of knowing the way.

The 3Ds

The Second D: Discipline

Are you prepared for the discipline of staying on the path?

In the previous chapter we explored common distractions that might lure you off your path. These included: concealed victimhood, avoidance, stagnation, rumination and overwhelm, saviour complex and exhaustion.

In this section, we will explore the kinds of disciplines you can call on to serve you as you walk your path. I have identified four primary disciplines that are worth cultivating during your time of transition to authentic practice:

○ longing
○ risk
○ trust
○ agreements.

Longing

You are longing to act on your own behalf. You are longing to be heard. You are longing to live your authentic self in the world. It is time to share your perspective and your message with the world. Longing is your summons to action.

To be heard you need to take action. The alternative is sounding like a broken record playing over and over with no-one interested in listening. I've been there. It's agony. The risk of taking action for your longing is nothing compared to the awfulness of feeling stuck in your own life.

The reality is your clients need your approach. They need your guidance. They yearn for your message and your touch. Someone, many someones, are waiting for you to deliver your service, so that they can receive it.

Act on your longing.

Risk

No two ways about it, acting on your longing for authentic practice is a risk. A guaranteed risk. When I opened my home-based practice and leased a space, at the time I felt it was way beyond my capacity. I was starting from scratch in a new loca-tion (which happened to be posh – the daughter of mining giant

Gina Rinehart was across the road from me). I had no idea how I was going to cover my rent, let alone build a home-based practice. The risk seemed real. It *was* real. So I decided to sub-lease one of the rooms.

Once I signed the lease, magical moments began to emerge. The universe provided clear guidance. For example, a friend stepped forward with guidance on setting up a functional interior in my clinic space. Her input solidified my thinking and fortified my trust.

Trust

As you find your path up what might feel like a mountain, you will begin to *know* there is an inner trust guiding you, an inner truth that only you can know. Your task is to simultaneously trust it – and question it. It is not an easy journey. It can at times be hard. It is not beyond you. It is an emotional rollercoaster. You will experience moments of exasperation and perhaps sheer terror, matched only by moments of exhilaration and wonder. At all times, you need to summon your inner resources to keep control. This is not the control of rigidity, inflexibility and fear. It is control as self-mastery.

The control of self-mastery facilitates and nourishes your trust as you build your practice.

Agreements

The control of self-mastery is sustained by agreements you make with yourself to govern your self-discipline. In this way, you will also cultivate skills inherent to self-discipline as you work towards opening, building and cultivating your practice.

Thus are the elements of The Second D: Discipline. Discipline will keep you on your path as make your way up the mountain face.

§

Desire, opportunity and belief

The time will come when your reality evolves, and you no longer care about the status quo. As you walk your path and navigate the challenges transformation asks from you, you will find you have your own rhythm, your own style, your own way of working. You will claim the different perspectives you bring to your practice. You realise you have a philosophical approach *and* the courage to share your ideas. You no longer feel a need to justify what you are doing or how you are feeling. You know what you have is enough.

This is your time.

This is your time to trust, your time to fulfill the promise of the idea birthed in you. This promise is your new opportunity, for yourself and your clients. When fear surfaces, with experience you discover it's easy enough to convince yourself out of it — because you *know* your fear has no substance, that you are frightened of the unknown path and that is just like being frightened of fear itself. Through this process you will discover the unknown is to be embraced. It is your ally, your guide, your trusted companion.

The moment you start your authentic practice is the moment you embody true ownership of your genius. You may have danced with it before; however, back then it was an idea. Now your genius has form in the world. This is the moment you also realise the enormity of the power of your inner strength. You trust you have all you need to keep walking the path. You know there are risks involved. You have learned to keep walking with clear-eyed intent. You have understood that regardless of how challenging and risky things feel, that the wheel turns and everything will be fine. You know how to accept that risks are involved and they are scary and they are inherent in the transformational journey. To act on your longing is to step into the unknown. No risk = no transformation. No trust = no transformation. This journey requires self-discipline, and it is underpinned by agreements you make or have made with yourself.

The longing–risk–trust triad

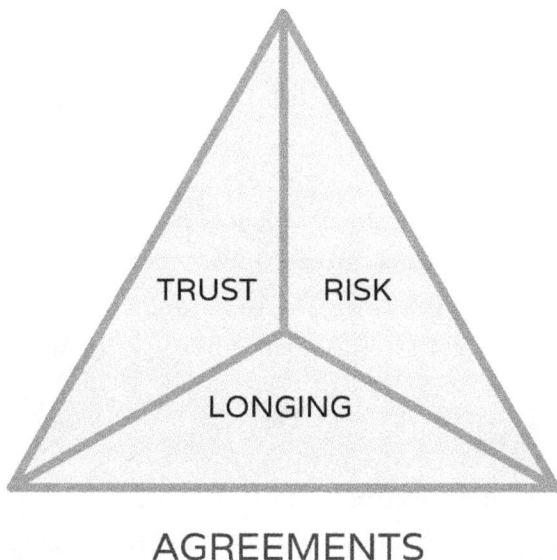

The longing-risk-trust triad is a pictorial representation of the elements inherent to setting up your practice. Held by trust, you are aware of the risks in taking action for your longing for authentic practice. The triad components will stretch and compress you. This is represented by the triangle. Mechanically, when you place a load on one side of the triangle, that side stretches whilst the other two sides simultaneously compress, allowing the triangle to maintain its shape. This is natural law. This is why the triangle is the strongest shape. For our purposes, it represents the mountain you need to climb. The triangle's capacity for stretching and compressing are the same forces required to form the mountain itself – the universe is with you as you climb.

The thought of climbing a mountain from base to peak can be daunting. *And a little or a lot exciting.* The incline makes it doable. Of course it's challenging – a steep incline can be a deterrent not to be tackled, or it is simply a hurdle between you and the promise of the summit. Tackling the mountainside will teach you endurance, and this brings forth moments of magic. It is, after all, only when you are out of your comfort zone that you exhilarate in magic moments that, in right timing along the way, *will save your life.* It could be another climber that comes from nowhere and offers help, not to be seen on the path again; or a little bird that breaks the lonely silence with a chirp, and sees you in ways that transfer much-needed information.

This is surrender to natural law.

The longing-risk-trust triad is living in natural law.

❧

The desire-opportunity-belief triad

There needs to be healthy tension between longing, risk and trust for growth to occur. Once you acknowledge the tension between risk and longing, you have what you need to evolve your consciousness and understand that your risk is in fact an inborn desire. It is your birthright to do good for yourself and the world. Risk has transformed into endless opportunities. Each situation you encounter along the way is a stepping stone of opportunity that reinforces trust. This trust is unwavering belief. Your belief will allow you to see calm in the storm, every time. With belief you are buffeted against illusions of time and the distractions of other people's opinions. With belief you are unattached to outcomes.

The desire-opportunity-belief triad corresponds directly to the longing-risk-trust triad. A representation of this is as follows:

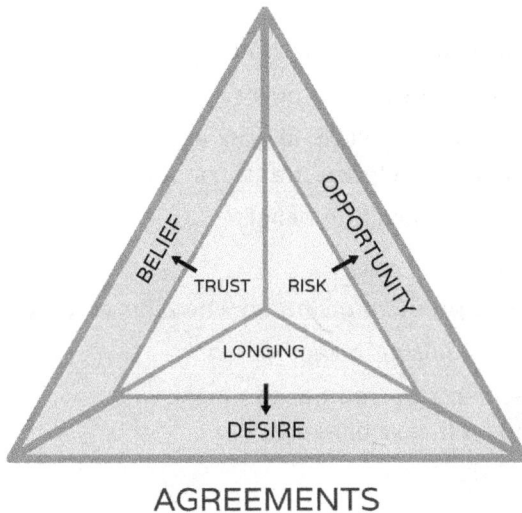

AGREEMENTS

Natural law: Correspondence 4

Trusting the unwalked/unfamiliar path can be challenging.

As you immerse yourself in the following exercises, I encourage you to reflect on other potent times in your life where you longed for something, took the risks involved, and trusted yourself to see it through.

Transitional Moment
Exploring the Triads

Longing–risk–trust triad

What risks do you fear in actioning the call to your authentic practice?

Which of these risks are 'real' and which are simply fear itself?

What is asked from you to address the risks that are real?
Reflect upon your capacity for trusting the unknown.
Reflect upon your capacity for trusting yourself. Write down examples where you have and have not.

Desire–opportunity–belief triad

What previous risks do you now see as opportunities?

Remember to strike a POSE to walk yourself through the perceived risks to help you transform into opportunity.

What are your unwavering beliefs?

Agreements

When are you prone to giving up when things get difficult?

What is your capacity to keep going?

What agreements do you need to make with yourself to sustain your self-discipline?

5

BRIGHT AND BEAUTIFUL

The previous chapter addressed the necessity of fuelling your own fire and owning your genius. As well, so far we have explored two of The 3Ds – Discernment and Discipline. The third and final D – Delivery – is the current that runs through the next two chapters. Delivery is simultaneously the task at hand and the path ahead. Before we address Delivery head on, it's important to turn and face two elephants in the room:

1. instant gratification
2. the long haul.

These elephants are counterpoints to each other, one – instant gratification – programmed to undermine the other, the long haul. The long haul is a sober reality that you best face right now. Once we've briefly explored these elephants, we'll move on to the most important stabilising factors that will serve you for the long haul: money, communication, labour, time, networking, and cost of living – all of which are pivotal to your capacity for Delivery.

Tending to these elemental forces now will ensure you are well-positioned for navigating the world you're creating. These forces are the steady road beneath your feet, supporting you to cycle through the longing-risk-trust triad in tandem with

The 3Ds, whilst keeping your spirits intact. Even when you feel like you're losing your way, you will learn to keep your spirits raised, bright and beautiful.

Instant gratification

Prior to 2014 I was the epitome of instant gratification. The fact is I did not know any better. I grew up seeking emotional highs. As a young adult I fed this obsession by jumping from one learning seminar to another. Even though I met the teacher who would transform my life path in 2006, it was a good decade before I began to practice her teachings. Interestingly, this was the same point at which I began teaching her work myself.

Before this time my mind had been a stuck record: I needed to 'be in the know', I perpetually feared 'missing out', I didn't want to 'be the odd one out'. Eventually I stopped obsessing over 'the latest thing', and I gave up prioritising the 'need to make money' and 'I need to make it big like everyone else'. Phew.

The fact is, instant gratification is fleeting. It is not sustainable. As fabulous as the emotional highs are at the time, highs come with lows and they will wear you out. One of the great challenges in setting up your authentic practice will be overcoming your particular version of instant gratification.

The long haul

On the other hand, contrary to instant gratification, the long haul can feel boring and/or uneventful and/or monotonous and/or … and so on. Committing to the long haul may initially feel tiresome. It is likely your goals will feel out of reach.

The long haul is systematic by nature. It is steady. And yet, it is in this perceivably uneventful place you will find your foundation stones, the bedrock beneath your authentic practice, the scaffolding that holds you up and frames your world as you find your perfect inner place from which to Deliver, authentic in practice and in life.

Let me lift this weight off your shoulders.

The long haul is being comfortable with yourself and your practice. It provides the foundation you need for creating your life. To get to the long haul – to Deliver on the promise of your vision – you will need to start thinking about the following themes in a new light: money, communication, labour, time, networking, and cost of living.

What follows are action steps you might consider as you prepare to Deliver. These are foundational tools that could have saved me a lot of time and angst if I'd had the wherewithal to apply them right from the beginning. As it is, you can learn from my learnings. And over time you will adapt them to your own ways of being and authentic practice.

∽

Forecasting and insights

There are two areas in your life in which you may not yet have established yourself in steady rhythm – money and time. The following is a training opportunity to reset your money and time patterns, and exchange potentially destructive behaviours for clarity in these areas.

Money

You are establishing a practice – stand by to learn numerous lessons about money. It comes with the territory. Conscious and unconscious money patterns that impact, hinder and shape your financial wellbeing will rise and threaten to bite you. Unless you have inherited significant sums of money, poor money management can devour you, boots and all. These conscious and unconscious patterns *must* be disentangled from your energetic systems if you are to grow a successful business. You may not eliminate them all together, you must, however, learn to recognise them and take radical action before they do.

Money *management* is the key to the long haul. It is the literal measure of your progress. You will go through periods of feeling as if you have made no progress at all, which is why I'm sharing with you the measuring tool I use to this day to assess my business wellbeing.

That measuring tool is a money distribution system. I promise you, it will become your new most stable and trustworthy best friend. This tool is rewarding, and it allows you at any time to confidently know where you have come from and where you are going.

During the development of my own practice, I followed the advice and guidance of financial experts and read books on money mindset. I have combined the ideas I have gleaned from the books and experts into a financial management discipline that has served me well for the past ten years.

Money Distribution Process – MDP

My Money Distribution Process works like magic. Why 'magic'? because when you action the money distribution, you are able to measure and assess your financial status, voilà, magic.

Instant gratification is the enemy of the MDP. Instant gratification undermines your financial wellbeing, and while the long haul may seem slow, remember *it's systematic.* It is steady. You may perceive it as boring, yet it is the most rewarding foundational financial step you can implement as you embark on the practice journey.

In my early 20s I wanted to travel overseas. At that time, a 'world ticket' was the most economical way to fly around the world, clockwise or anticlockwise. Being my first sizeable purchase, a couple of thousand dollars, I knew I needed to save. These were pre-digital banking days. I was paid in cash. I got myself a money box. Every time I received my wage, I placed the majority of the cash, big and small notes, in the money box. I saved rigorously for more than nine months. I was living with my parents, which meant I did not need to pay for my keep. The time came to open my money box and calculate my savings. It amounted to just over $2600. This exercise gave me first-hand experience of saving, and the rewards that follow it.

The MDP is the process of regularly distributing 100% of your income to various specifically-allocated bank accounts. It is just like saving for an old-fashioned holiday, although now we are allocating your salary for other fun things such as expenses, rent, tax and super. This establishes a financial rhythm in your life and gives you a clear, ongoing measurement of your business's financial performance. This discipline will clear your mind and boost your confidence as you take the next steps to evolving your practice.

I recommend committing to the Money Distribution Process of measurement for a minimum of one year. This is enough time to evolve a system that is aligned with your growing business. This system enables you to know precisely where your money is and where it went. This makes money one less thing to think about and it will take a huge weight off your shoulders.

There are three steps in the Money Distribution Process:

1. create a series of specifically-allocated bank accounts (as per further instructions below) and title the names accordingly (as per further instructions below).
2. transfer money in pre-set percentages to each account. Set up a regular transfer time for efficiency and ease.
3. write a series of reminders to put in your calendar for actioning.

The following diagram offers an overview of the Money Distribution Process.

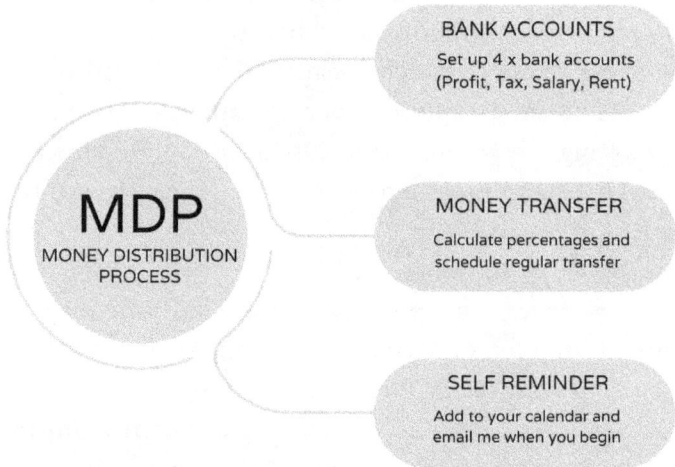

Money Distribution Process

MDP
MONEY DISTRIBUTION
PROCESS

BANK ACCOUNTS
Set up 4 x bank accounts
(Profit, Tax, Salary, Rent)

MONEY TRANSFER
Calculate percentages and
schedule regular transfer

SELF REMINDER
Add to your calendar and
email me when you begin

Comprehensive explanations for each step in the Money Distribution Process is as follows:

MDP Step 1: create a series of bank accounts

First, establish a business bank account.

This ensures all your business transactions, income and expenses flow through one account. In this way you will know at all times the financial and tax status of your business. Remember, we're streamlining and simplifying a process that can quickly deteriorate into chaos. Your peace of mind is more important than your resistance to a business bank account.

Then, in addition to your business account, set up four free everyday transactional online bank accounts. Rename your bank accounts as follows:

○ rename the business account Expenses
○ rename the four everyday accounts Profit, Tax, Salary and Rent.

You will regularly allocate set percentages of income to each of these accounts.

You may think you have your savings under control. You may think you have your business finances under control. However, odds are there are pitfalls in your illusion. If any of the following statements applies to you, I suggest you implement this exercise yesterday:

- you don't seem to have money to spend as you like
- cost of living is high
- you have a credit card for your business
- you are scared to look at your bank balance
- you do not know the exact amount of your monthly income
- you do not know the exact amount of your monthly expenses
- you cannot tell me how much money you have to spend on whatever you want
- you are resisting this exercise
- you are not up to date with your taxes
- you are seeing 20 or fewer clients a week.*

Secondly, rename your business account Expenses. Your business account – renamed Expenses – is for paying all your business expenses. It is solely for business expenses. From this account you will pay your bills, supplies, amenities, seminars, equipment, any and all expenses related to your business will come from this account.

All the money that you earn is channelled first into this account, and it is from this account you will transfer to the everyday accounts. This account tracks your income, providing

---

* Please note, I am not a financial advisor. I am simply sharing my way of managing income and expenses in ways that I know are helpful. I spent years trying to figure out how I could implement viable ways of managing money. I have been exactly where you are. Everything on the list above has applied to me at some time. The MDP process calmed me. It ensured my mind was free to focus on the evolution of my business free from financial confusion.

a decent measure for knowing how much money *actually* came in. You will be surprised how much money flows through your hands in the months and years ahead, and – if you resist the Money Distribution Process – even more surprised by how much money you let slip through your fingers because you failed to allocate it to its appropriate bank account.

Thirdly, commit to maintaining your everyday accounts: Profit, Tax, Salary, Rent.

Your Profit account is where you store your profit. The purpose of this account is to easily calculate how much income has entered the business.

The purpose of your Tax account is right there in its name. Don't get caught out at tax time. Put away for your tax so you don't sweat it when tax time comes around, which it will with monotonous regularity. I have fallen in love with this account. It is a joy. Because having money to pay my taxes means I've earned a good income *and* there's always some left over I can choose to spend.

I know two practitioners who avoided their taxes – one for 11 years and the other for 22 years. I am not joking. Their lives became a taxation nightmare. Please do not be that practitioner. If you are, contact an accountant or email me and we can chat about how to get you back on track. Life is much, much better without taxation headaches – I promise.

The Salary account is to make sure you give yourself a salary. The income that comes in is just that: money coming in. It is not your salary. There is great satisfaction in giving yourself a salary. It is also your wake-up call. *You* own and run the practice; the practice does not own and run you. There are many financial advisers who remind you to pay yourself first. I implemented this practice, and it has given me incredible freedom.

The Rent account ensures you have the money you need to

pay one of the most important foundation stones of your business. Yes, even if your practice may be at home. *And*, if you work from home this means you will cover the cost of your business's usage.

When I started out, I was sharing a house with my sisters. I did not pay additional rent because for my office space as I didn't think I had to; and besides, I didn't have money to pay rent (this was before I implemented the Money Distribution Process). My sisters did not appreciate my home-based practice and, obviously, it was rude of me not to contribute to the rent whilst solely utilising the office space. At the time, however, I was so focused on trying to figure out how to run a practice I failed to pay attention to my responsibilities.

MDP Step 2: transfer money in pre-set percentages to each account

There are two parts to this process:

○ diary commitment
○ percentage transfer.

Diary commitment

It is important that you set a regular time in your diary for your bank account transfers. This rhythm can be daily, weekly or monthly. I recommend you start with weekly transfers. For example, Fridays at 3pm or Mondays at 11am. Set this time in stone.

When I started my Money Distribution Process, I transferred the allocations daily. I was obsessive about it, and secretly excited. I learned the hard way that this ate up valuable time and energy, and soon became a rollercoaster ride of stress. You are welcome to learn from my mistake.

Set a weekly time in your diary for bank account transfers and commit to it.

Percentage transfer

Percentage transfer is the most important aspect of the MDP. This is because you are going to learn what you do with your money. This practice may also trigger your greatest resistance – I know it did for me – as you face the reality that your expenses may outrun your income.

The amount of money you transfer to your accounts is going to be a percentage amount, not a monetary amount. The reason for this is that 100% of the income needs to be distributed into the other accounts for this process to be effective.

It is important to note the Money Distribution Process is not about savings, nor about putting money aside for a rainy day. Its purpose is to understand how much money flows through your business, and to offer you a readily accessible measuring tool for assessing how you are travelling at any given point in time.

You are allocating what comes into your hands so that you understand your worth.

Honouring your home

If you are working from home, assess approximately how much of your home is occupied by your office/clinic room. For example, measure your entire house's square meterage and your practice room square meterage, divide the room from your house to give you a percentage. If 10% of your home is used for your clinic room, then 10% of your expenses will be transferred to your Rent account.

Alternatively, choose to put aside a regular amount for the rent, for example $50 a week, $80 a week or $150 a week. In this way you will be honouring your home, your workspace, yourself and others who share your home. If you live by yourself and pay rent, talk to your accountant about whether this can be classified as a business expense and tax deduction.

Suggested percentages transfer based on the rental example above are:

- Expenses account = 60% of the money that came in is left in this account
- Profit account = 1% transfer
- Tax account = 20% transfer
- Salary account = 19% transfer
- Rent account = dollar sum transfer from your Expenses account.

To clarify, 60% of your income is left in your Expenses account. It is recommended that the percentages you allocate to the other accounts be determined by the dollar amount. By all means, modify the percentages to suit your circumstances. The only percentage I recommend you avoid changing is the 1% profit. I shall explain why in a moment.

To recap, every dollar of income you earn is to be distributed from your Expenses account into one of the four everyday accounts.

The following table gives you an overview of sample percentage transfers.

Accounts	Percentage Allocation	Weekly Income Amount	
		$640.00	*$2300.00*
		Amount Distributed	
Profit	1%	$6.40	$23.00
Expenses	60%	$384.00	$1380.00
Tax	20%	$128.00	$460.00
Salary	19%	$121.60	$437.00
Rent	*Weekly transfer from expenses*		
Total Allocation	100%	$640.00	$2300.00

If your income is $640 for the week, and you distribute the money to your everyday accounts according to the percentages above: your profit is $6.40, your expenses will be $384, the amount to put aside for tax is $128 and your salary is $121.60. You will deduct your rent from the $384 you have left in the Expenses account.

If your income was $2300 for the week, this translates to profit $23, expenses $1380, tax $460 and salary $437. You will deduct your rent from Expenses account.

Why 1% for profit?

Simply put, 1% is easy to track. It is an amount that does not involve stretching your expenses to the limit, and it is an easy number to glance at and multiply. For instance, if you have accumulated $60 in your Profit account, you know that $6000 flowed through your hands: 1% of $6000 = $60. If you have accumulated $700 in your Profit account, you know that $70,000 from your practice has flowed through your hands.

This 1% is also sneaky. It is sneaky because you think it is a low amount. It is sneaky because it is tempting to think you can turn it into savings and squirrel away 5% or 10% or more. I want to remind you that this percentage is your tracker. It is your tool. It is **not** your savings account. I have implemented this 1% strategy for ten years and I have not touched the money in this account. I have made the account non-visible so that I am not tempted to touch it. I get annual paper statements and this is the only time all year that I look at it. If only you knew how much money had flowed through my hands during ten years of practicing – it surprises even me.

To reiterate – do not get caught in the trap of thinking that 1% is nothing, and do not touch this account. It is only to put money into, so that you can measure and enjoy the experience of your money flow.

Implement these actions and experience the results for yourself. Decide whether you will transfer weekly, fortnightly or monthly. Experiment, find the rhythm that works for you.

MPD Step 3: write reminders for actioning money distribution

This step is straightforward: add money transfer time reminders to your calendar. Choose your day and time for setting up reminders for yourself to distribute money from your Expenses account to your everyday accounts. Put this action step in your calendar and *then do the actual action.*

Once you have set up your accounts, email me at therese@ artofchiropractic.com.au In the subject heading write: *The Money Distribution Process has started.* In the body of the message, let me know the percentages you have allocated to your bank accounts, and the day and time of your regular transfer.

If you are working as a contractor in someone else's clinic, there is a high chance that no-one is paying a contribution into your superannuation, unless you are. When you start to practise on your own, you will pay your own superannuation. Most practitioners put superannuation in a little box in the back of their mind and forget about it. Superannuation is the money employers put aside on your behalf so that when you retire, you have money to live well. There are many online resources telling you how much money you should have in your super account. A quick internet search for 'how much money should I have in my super' will return many tables advising you based on your age and gender how much super you should have. If you are your own boss, put money aside into your superannuation. For those in the USA, Superannuation Contribution in Australia is equivalent to your 401K.

Take action today. Register with a superannuation fund and place 15% of your salary in to your super account on a regular basis. Start now.

Accounts	Percentage Allocation	Weekly Income Amount	
Salary		$121.60	$437.00
Super (401K)	15% Distributed from your salary	($18.24)	($65.55)

Natural law: Correspondence 5

This section focused on money – the next section focuses on time. This section has been devoted to setting you up for long haul authentic business success. If you are resisting the MDP that's okay. You don't have to do what I say – but I am curious as to your reasoning. Perhaps you have a system that works brilliantly for you – please, share it with me, I'd love to hear from you. Perhaps you feel resistance? Perhaps your money worries have risen like a tidal wave and are threatening to swamp you.

Whatever actions you implement to manage your money, the important thing is understanding and recognising the difference between instant gratification and the long haul. There may be many areas of your life that swing between instant gratification and the long haul. Watch for them, be ready when they surface.

Transitional Moment
Instant Gratification, the Long Haul, and the Money Distribution Process

Instant Gratification

What gives you instant gratification?

What are your patterns for seeking instant gratification, emotional highs and resistant to the long haul?

Money Distribution process

Write down your understanding of the benefits of the Money Distribution Process.

Are you resisting the Money Distribution Process? If so, why?

Are you willing to explore your money patterns?

Do you have a superannuation account you are contributing to?

Time

Time action categories

Time management is key to developing clear focus in your practice, and, just as importantly, it will set you up for the good life outside your practice. By observing the following Time Action Categories you will avoid chaos, burnout and stress, and enjoy clarity in your daily practice priorities. You need another reason why? So you are in control of your practice, and your practice is not controlling you.

In our cyclical natural world, western human time is linear. When we adhere to linear time, *as if it is real*, it is easy to forget that we are part of a universe of cycles, and that we have cycles too. As with the tides that rise and fall, the sun that rises and sets, the moon that swells and grows dark, you too rise, shine and rest. As with the tides, the sun and the moon, there are many life aspects we cannot control. We can, however, develop a sense of order that will help us to control those things that are ours to control in our own orbit. This, in turn, will grow confidence in our capacity for expressing ourselves in our clinic.

To develop this sense of order we must understand what we do with our time.

As with the Money Distribution Process, time needs to be allocated, and we will use percentages to make these allocations. This enables you to understand:

○ how you utilise your time
○ whether or not you are on track to sustaining good business, clinical and personal health and wellbeing.

As with money, this too is part of your long haul strategy. It may leave you anticipating boredom and uneventfulness. Trust me. The Time Action Categories provide steadiness and clarity to your working rhythm. If you are willing to apply Discipline to the Time Action Categories you will generate *in you* enormous power.

The Time Action Categories are for you if any of the following is relevant to you:

o you do not have set hours in your practice
o there is too much idle time and space in your day
o you're thinking of getting a side job because that is all you can think to do to 'save' you (from boredom, stress, financial woe etc)
o you're stewing on the idea that going out on your own was a bad idea
o you're making house calls when you do not want to.

As with universal cycles, your authentic practice will also experience waves of highs and lows. It is easy to be lazy, or let the discipline of your home/business routine slide. To help you build stable foundations for yourself as a businesswoman and as a practitioner, I have developed the Time Action Categories as a resource for measuring your time. This will stabilise your business foundations and give you the freedom you need to create and explore new aspects of your clinical and personal life.

Time Action Categories remind you that you are in for the long haul, not instant gratification. The Time Action Categories are subsets of your practice time. These subsets are: admin time, service time and strategy time.

The following time allocation strategy is based on a 40-hour week in the clinic. You may choose to allocate less than 40 hours a week for your clinic, in which case calculate accordingly.

One's own time = self time

We will address one's own time – self time – first. This is for one main reason: no you, no practice.

In the initial stages of working in your practice, you will likely have momentum. There is the buzz of setting up your practice, the highs of accomplishment and achievement. Once the buzz wears off, you may experience periods where business is slow.

Even though this is part of the natural practice cycle, the slowness can challenge your self-confidence. As you build your practice, you may experience a lot of time between clients, or you might get bored. You may even lose interest in the project altogether.

When things slow down, you may start telling yourself that running your own practice was not a good idea. You may worry there isn't enough money coming in. You might start looking for other jobs. This idle, inactive, do-nothing time can destabilise your emotions and lead to negative self-talk that can mess with your mind.

As well, in your busy times you may experience aches and pains that seem to come from nowhere. This is a surefire indication that your body is pleading for a break. On top of this, the needs of your clients have the potential to exhaust you. Other people's energies can be draining in the healing space.

The reality is, if you don't take action to proactively protect your health and wellbeing, you're heading for a crisis. To avoid burnout, you *must* prioritise time for you: your thoughts, your ideas, your events, your areas of interest – anything that provides nourishing fulfillment for you.

Naturally, this is easier said than done. So think about how much time you need in a day, a week, to do the things you love or want to do. Commit to those times by putting them in the diary. Self time is the most important thing you can do for business, your clients and you. Get creative on how you fill your self time, and add plenty of fun activities in there.

Self time is not negotiable.

Admin time

Admin time is for administration tasks. You are a clinical practitioner. You are not an admin specialist. Therefore, in the spirit of self-preservation, admin time can be considered tasks someone else can do. These tasks include: paying bills, stock refills, paperwork, cleaning, washing towels, social media, watering plants, updating intake forms, emails, and so on.

If you do not have enough work or the financial resources for someone else to do admin task, put time aside, perhaps four hours once a week to complete admin duties. Admin time is strictly admin time. In admin time you pay bills, make phone calls, reply to emails, water plants and so on.

Service time

Service Time is the time it takes for provision of your services in exchange for money. If you do not have clients booked in, use the time to talk to potential clients, networking, distributing flyers, walking around chatting to local businesses, offering yourself as speaker to local community groups, and so on. In other words, if you are not seeing clients, service time can still be utilised for generating new clients *in exchange for money*.

I repeat: service time is the provision of your services in exchange for money. It is the work of your business. The key phrase is *in exchange for money*. This is a warning against trading your services for other services, which can be especially tempting if your client numbers are low. For example, I treat you and you treat me in exchange, or you give me a hair cut in exchange for a treatment from me. No.

No. No. No.

Until you have established your business, treat your practice with the respect it deserves. Pay for your services, just as you would like to be paid for your services.

I charge all practitioners and all clients who come to my clinic. I do not give a discount. This ensures I give my clients the professional attention they deserve, and it prevents me from delivering a half-arsed or even resentful job if I'm tired. Payment keeps me on track.

You want service time to be 80% of your practice time.

Strategy time

Strategy time is the game changer. This is your ideas' generation time. I allocate four hours a week for strategy time. Thanks to strategy time, I am writing this book and sharing my practice experiences and my message. Thanks to strategy time, I am doing what I am truly inspired to do.

Strategy time includes sitting and thinking up ideas, and investigating ideas that inspire you. At first I found strategy time challenging. It was painful and hard. Many times I sat through my allocated strategy time doing nothing at all. Yet I persisted. *I learned to strategise.* Eventually, my persistence resulted in:

o the introduction of new programs for my clients
o wonderful workshops that I still facilitate
o writing and delivering speeches about subjects that matter to me.

And now a new project: writing a book about a subject dear to my heart, on themes that I have interested in, have experience with and I'm passionate about.

Thinking through time

How do you best allocate time to your Time Action Categories?

Start by thinking carefully about how many hours you want to work – in a day? a week? The question is not what you think you *need* to work to have a successful business, nor what you *have* to work to make a steady income. Rather, how many hours do you genuinely want to work in a day and/or a week?

My happy space is four hours in a row in a day. After four hours I become grumpy, I lose focus. This is unfair on my clients and unfair on me. So I work in four-hour chunks, and then have a very big break.

Decide how many days you will work in your practice. One day? Three days? Five days? Your Time Action Categories are allocated within your practice days.

You want 80% of your practice time to be service time. This maximises your earning potential. After that, share your time equally between admin time and strategy time, that is, 10% to each.

For example, my work practice hours use to be Monday afternoons, Tuesday mornings and afternoon – with a four-hour gap in between, Wednesday evening, Thursday early morning and Friday morning.

Admin time was scheduled for four hours on Monday morning, prior to opening my clinic. Strategy time was scheduled for four hours on Friday afternoons. I did not put scheduling boundaries on replying to appointment requests on my phone. If someone texted something *practice-related* and I read it, I would reply. I did put boundaries on my emails, replying daily at 11am and 3pm only.

My time management breakthrough came with *knowing* what I was doing with my time. I invite you to reflect on how you spend your time, and how you consume your time in your practice.

Self-accountability is essential for practice success.

Time action categories

There is a total of 168 hours in a week, every week. The following graph is calculated on a 40-hour work week.

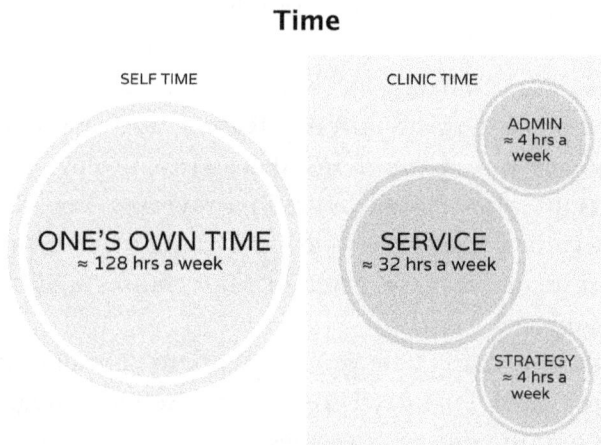

Time

SELF TIME   CLINIC TIME

ADMIN
≈ 4 hrs a
week

ONE'S OWN TIME
≈ 128 hrs a week

SERVICE
≈ 32 hrs a week

STRATEGY
≈ 4 hrs a
week

Natural law: Correspondence 5

Time is fleeting. There is much to be experienced and much enjoyment to be had in life. It can be easy to let your practice consume your time and your joy. I invite you to explore where and how you are allocating and spending your time, and reflect on ways of allocating time in order to maximise your joy *and* your profits.

Transitional Moment
Time

Service Time

Do you get exhausted from your clinic work? If so, what contributes to your exhaustion?

Do you have a joy period in your practice? If so, what is the duration of hours or minutes before your joy diminishes?

How many hours a week do you want to work in clinic?

Do you feel pressured to work more hours in clinic that you'd like?

How can you overcome this pressure?

How can striking a POSE assist you to act authentically for yourself and your clinic?

Self Time

List the activities you do - and would like to do - in your self time.

Strategy Time

How will you spend your strategy time today?

Are there strategies you know you need to undertake and yet you resist? List them.

6

INVISIBLE INFRASTRUCTURE

In the previous chapter we tended to practical business basics. We will now turn our attention to internalised invisible infrastructure that is likely to encroach on your momentum. This chapter addresses lifeworld frameworks *in you* that shape and can potentially undermine your vision. Chapter 6 offers simple action plans for guiding you through potentially sticky and stuck places as you build your practice.

જ

Renewal patterns

My friendship trajectory changed when I enrolled in chiropractic studies and stepped into a new world. I was learning new information and new subjects of enormous interest to me. There was a consequence to this: the slow destruction of my previous self, and, eventually, the demise of long-held friendships. My interests changed. My conversational subjects changed. I changed.

I was initially hurt by the loss of my everyday friends. I felt isolated, and ill-prepared to journey on alone. The love and care I felt for my friends was not diminished by the slow drift of my change in direction and availability.

I understand now that this was honest expression of a simple pattern of renewal, whereby in order for something new to come into creation, something else had to die. It is natural law, and I was not exempt. Creation and destruction come hand in hand. When you create life, you also create death. When you build something, it also means what you build can be knocked down.

As you step forward to create your new practice, you are seeing through the end of your previous ways of being. You are transitioning from one way of being to another. Some transitions are easy, liberating. Other transitions may feel like your world is falling apart.

In creating your practice, you are sowing the seeds of destruction of your previous self. If you hinder the destruction, if you refuse to move forward with the tides of change into the new world that awaits you, if you cling to old ways whilst reaching for new ways – you will become a wreck. Here's what hindering your destruction may look like:

- opening your practice and then talking yourself out of it
- hanging out with friends who you know you no longer want to hang around with
- looking at other people instead of minding your own business
- being negatively impacted by small and unnecessary challenges
- not doing activities you know you want and need to do
- being scared to try something different
- experiencing resistance to new ideas, new people, new environments – all the wonders and promises of your new world will remain out of reach.

This phase of destruction of your known self and known world can seem catastrophic. Yet it need not be violent. It is likely to be enlivening, to be sure, and at times sad, to be sure, however there are strategies you can put in place to support you and those around you to gently navigate your new world. To manage this transition well, you will need to set standards and put protocols in place for responding to situations as they arise. In this way, rather than being beholden to ways of being that no longer serve you, you will move forward with ease and grace.

I would like to share with you experiences of navigating my own patterns of renewal, followed by sample standards and protocols I implemented. You will notice my standards and protocols are straightforward and limited in number. This is because I needed to be able to apply them in the midst of juggling the demands of change and the needs of my new business. Keeping them few and straightforward ensured I was not overwhelmed by my own standards and protocols.

Put up the sign: navigating patterns of renewal

By the time I had finished being an associate in someone else's practice I was miserable. I wanted nothing to do with other practitioners. It was as if my heart had been wrenched open, and pulled out from me. I had grown accustomed to observing myself as an empty shell, no longer alive to the light that once danced in me. I was crushed. I longed for my light to shine. And I made a vow to myself: my light would no longer be dimmed.

I opened my own home-based practice, and this opened a new world to me. New people came into my life. I experienced authentic connections with practitioners who were like-minded – because, and only because, *I* started being authentic.

I trusted myself. I believed in my way of working. I acted on my desire, I acted on the opportunities for everything for change, I believed in the unknown that something else would come – I trusted myself, for only I could take this step. This is not to suggest we control outcomes. It was just that for me, the need to take the opportunity of working for myself, and trust the urgency of the moment to leave everything that was familiar, had become greater than my willingness to remain stuck and miserable.

Watching old patterns linger

That leap into change, as I mentioned above, came at the price of old friendships that were holding me back from my new world. I cannot tell you how many times I fought this change.

How many times have you been caught in the same trap, and promised yourself you will not do the same thing again? "Next time I will do this differently," you say, only to find yourself again in the same situation. Foresight is better than hindsight. So as a way of shortcutting your transitional traps, let me introduce you to one of my many excuses for explaining away one of my particular habitual traps:

When I first opened my home-based practice, I wanted to put a big banner outside saying: "Taking New Bookings." A mentor had suggested this to me. She knew that the banner would bring in new clients. I shared my banner intentions with a person who was not the best person to share it with. She questioned why I would put up such a sign, telling me in no uncertain terms that it was disrespectful to the neighbourhood.

And so I allowed this one minor opinion to impact me and hold me back. This conversation devastated my self-belief. In tears, I enrolled in a coaching session to rebuild my courage to display the sign.

It took another eighteen months before I felt worthy enough, strong enough, confident enough, to put up a sign outside my home-based practice only for it to be taken down a few months later because I was relocating.

It is important to note here that the other person was not the problem in this story. The problem was that I was seeking guidance from someone who had no affinity with the new world

I was creating for myself. She could only respond to me from the old place, from the world she lived in. The trouble was, I no longer shared her world.

The fact of the matter is that considering what other people will think of me has had a limiting hold on me for my entire life. It destroys me to the point of wrecking everything I know to be true and wonderful about myself. In the early days of setting up my home-based practice, those old patterns lingered like haunting ghosts, the Ghost of Other People's Opinions.

I invite you to put up your sign. *Put your sign out*, metaphorically or otherwise. A large bold sign so big that people in the next state can see it. *This is my sign*. This is me. This is my offering. This is who I am and I am here, to serve you. Please, email me (therese@artofchiropractic.com.au) a photo of your sign – it will bring me much joy.

Restoration of balance

I had a meltdown over that sign. I wrecked myself over that sign. Yet I want to share with you the balance that occurred in my life once I finally decided to put out the sign – and how my neighbour helped.

My neighbour Tariu had much faith in my practice.

"Therese, why is your banner so low? We need to put your banner up high. We need to put it so that everyone can see. Therese, let me do it for you." Within moments Tariu had popped home and returned with a drill and a ladder and before I knew it my sign was waving high.

Did I receive Tariu's encouragement with ease and grace? No, I did not. I resisted his suggestion, my old patterns reemerging in my head. Yet thanks to Tariu, I had no time to blink, let alone resist, let alone argue. Tariu had that sign up high and proud without negative input from me.

A new standard, a new protocol

As a result of this experience, I set in place a standard that I hold to this day. It is simple, it is straightforward: when I have an inspired idea, I do not tell anyone about my intentions. I just do it. My thoughts and my actions are not up for question or opinion from others. They are to be acted upon.

From there I established a protocol: if I need help to act upon my idea, I will be selective about who I enlist to help me. And then if others want to step forward to assist me to action my inspiration, great. All hands on deck, but I am the captain of my ship.

Other standards I have set in my practice life include:

o I did not share that I was writing this book with anyone other than my writing coach prior to its publication (including my partner)

o I started sculpting lessons and did not share I was sculpting with anyone

o I bought a bee hive and did not share the fact I had a beehive with anyone

o I decided I was getting my boat licence and did not share with anyone I was getting my boat licence.

In all transitional destructions in life there will be balance. That, too, is natural law. As you navigate change, before you escalate the situation to wrecking status, make up your mind about what you're going to do, and then do it. Do not hinder destruction. To do so is to block your future potential. Rather, invite destruction in as you create a new world – and have standards and protocols set in place to head off your potential for wreck and ruin.

Disruptions and agitations

Unchecked, disruptions and agitations can ruin a perfectly good idea. Disruptions and agitations are bonded, they are a unit. Disruptions, undisciplined, will lead to agitations small and huge. At this stage in our explorations of invisible infrastructure, it's best you know your disruptions and agitations patterns.

Disruptions might be pleasant ways of avoiding tasks at hand or sub-consciously papering over aspects of your life with which you are perpetually unsatisfied. Agitations might be small annoyances with the potential to cause extreme damage.

Disruptions and agitations can rob you of your momentum. A new idea, a text, YouTube rabbit holes, online shopping, social media, a new love interest, comparing yourself to perceived competitors, workshops, seminars, a new book, cleaning, re-organising, smoking – in the context of building your practice, these are all potential disruptions and agitations. They might offer you timeout from the realities of the discipline required to establish your practice, but they will return with interest in the form of an increased burden of heaviness.

My habitual disruptor and agitator was my phone. In those early years I was constantly reaching for my phone, even during clinic time. However, my main disruption was continuous education. I was addicted to seminars. Clinical practice seminars, business seminars, personal development seminars. For ten years seminars dominated my life. And one day I realised I was paying good money for seminars, I was giving precious time to seminars, but I was not applying what I learned in seminars.

In that moment I understood the seminars were masking a void in my life, and the void was personal relationships – including, and most especially, with myself. Learning seminars had become my ultimate escape. I found it easy to study. I felt as if it was the only thing I knew how to do well. It was where I got my social highs and ego boosts about what I knew. The reality was that I did not know how to take care of myself.

Somewhere in 2017 a dear friend enquired: "You attend a lot of seminars Therese, how do you absorb all that you have learned? I don't know how you do it, it's incredible." Alarm bells rang in my head. My friend was right. Her question ignited a new discipline within me. I decided I would not attend any seminar for a full year. And I did just that. Again, I implemented a new standard for myself: pay attention to disruptions and agitations. They are masking a more important need. In this instance, the need for enriching personal relationships. My new standard was accompanied by a new protocol: no seminars.

Disruptions are edgy behaviour patterns. The standards we set fall under one simple umbrella: pay attention, know thyself. Agitations are antsy behaviours triggered by edgy behaviour patterns. The protocols we put in place are what we will do.

I created this new way with conviction, without fuss or drama. I knew it would be hard for me. It was hard – and I was willing.

When you are in solo practice, your disruptions and agita-tions will run unchecked under your radar. They will rarely be evident, until the first sign begins to surface: dissatisfaction. You may start to notice you don't have time to attend the hairdresser, or you forget to water your plants, you ignore the loose screw on your door, you and your circle of friends gossip rather than speak intelligently and compassionately with each other. Most notably, clients are not booking and your weeks look a lot like empty.

In my case, my disruptions and agitations could have been perceived as continuous research, or working on the business, when in reality those seminars were a subtle, shiny, hypnotic object that hid from me the realities of my personal life. Not being fulfilled in my relationships, and my relationship to myself, fuelled my self-doubt and ultimately became my biggest disruptor and agitator.

Being honest with yourself

I mentioned earlier that sources of disruption and agitation might be a new idea, a text, YouTube rabbit holes, online shopping, social media, a new love interest, comparing yourself to perceived competitors, workshops, seminars, a new book, cleaning, reorganising and smoking. The simple way to get honest about disruptions and potential sources of agitation is have a good hard look at where your money goes. Where do you spend your money?

Fast foods? Quick trips to the coffee shop? Another bottle of wine?

When my friend jolted me awake by asking what I learned in the seminars, I decided to list every single seminar I had attended. It was a fulfilling exercise. I learned that I had learned enough, and that I had all I needed to work with confidence in my chosen profession. This realisation empowered me as I pursued my practice vision. It gave me a new focus, and eliminated a dreadful (though well-meaning) source disruption and agitation. It was time to focus on me, so I did the only right thing to do: I took up sculpting.

৵

Natural law: Correspondence 6

I invite you to reflect on destructive patterns that have the potential to undermine your practice. You'll recall my own habitual destructive pattern of attending seminars. At the time I told myself I was learning and upskilling, when in fact I was anxious I was missing out on information, professional development and network connections. The reality is, I did not trust myself.

The success of your practice depends on you developing strong invisible infrastructure. This section is an invitation to identify and address destructive potential distractions waiting in the shadows, and prepare for the new creations that are waiting to ignite in you.

Transitional Moments
Distractions and Renewal Patterns

List your major habitual distractions and what protocols will you put in place to prevent or minimise the impact of your distractive patterns.

How many continual learning/self-development seminars have you attended in the last year?

Do you have a sign outside your clinic waving high?

ॐ

Sculpting my way to healing me

Strangely, I felt guilty about not attending particular business and health seminars. It was as if it had been a duty, part of my fabricated need for approval. So I had to figure out how to fill my time in ways that were not solely focussed on business or work. My whole identity was my business and my work.

There was one thing I had wanted to do for a long time: I was curious about sculpting, and I began attending clay classes. Clay comes from the earth. I found touching clay, working with clay, to be grounding. The sculpting class was a new beginning. I was allowing myself desires which in the past I would have denied.

If you are thinking – 'Therese, you attended another seminar' – you would be right. However, sculpting is not related to my business or my work. It is also way outside the health field. Sculpting was not concentrated on helping and healing others or accumulating knowledge to help others. This was time to heal me.

Willpower

Tending to self-healing time through sculpting allowed me to plant new seeds of self-discipline, something that used to fly out the door for me. Now that I had given myself a taste of self-care, I experienced a new trajectory. I abstained from attending work or business-related seminars for eighteen months, six months longer than my original resolution. It took willpower. It was not all smooth sailing.

Through willpower I was forced to face head-on my monstrous inner turmoil of self-judgement. It was as if I had been baptised in bondage to this chronic need to undermine myself. Thus the engagement of willpower ignited new conversations with myself that were kind and compassionate and enriching; conversations that gave me self-permission to explore anything at all I wanted to explore.

In this way I learned to associate self-discipline with self-care. The more I took care of myself, the greater my willpower. I was no longer depriving myself of me, and work was no longer the be all and end all of my life.

Unbeknownst to me, the decision to care for myself by sowing seeds of self-discipline brought forth the wildest adventure yet to come.

The wild adventure

Before I share the following sequence of events, I need to let you know that in 2016 I stayed up till three o'clock in the morning creating a vision board with pretty pictures. I had magazines splayed out around me as I snipped from them words and images that caught my attention.

I cut out an image of a map to represent travel. I remember thinking, 'I do not know where it is, I just want to represent travel.' I cut out rivers, waterfalls and boats, and images of presenters and business role models, including Richard Branson.

Two weeks later as I visited my local markets, where I noticed an older woman with grey hair, glasses and a beautiful smile standing at a table. Behind her was a big banner – with the same map I had on my vision board. Naturally, curiosity got the best of me. I beelined to the table and asked her:

"What is that map?"

She responded with a French accent: "It is the Camino."

I blurted out: "What is the Camino?"

She came to the front of the desk: "Camino de Santiago de Compostela, you have not heard of it?"

Still I did not understand. I noticed she was selling a book, titled *Boots To Bliss*.

"Is this your book?"

"Yes," she replied. "I walked eight hundred kilometres."

Now I understood. This was a hike. I thought 'what an accomplishment'. Then she introduced herself. She was Claude Tranchant. We chatted for while, and as we embraced to bid each other farewell she said, "The Camino is a pilgrimage."

Finally I understood. It was not a hike, it was *pilgrimage*. As my body embodied the whole heartedness of this, I broke into tears. She held me close. That hug transferred knowledge and wisdom to me that changed my world.

I had long thought pilgrimage was some stupid religious thing. When Claude hugged me I felt a big buzz. She woke me up. She caused me to listen: Shhh, pay attention: *I have to do this*.

I contacted my friend Katina.

"We need to do this thing called the Camino," I said.

"Yes," was her reply.

In January 2019 I decided I would extend my clinic lease in Brisbane for a further three years. I was not enthused with Brisbane. I did not like the climate but nonetheless, I wanted to prove to myself that I could make it on my own. See? *Still needing to prove myself.*

I sat down to write the email to the real estate agent, stating my preference for the lease extension, when I received an email from them asking me to consider ending the lease early. Their message took me by surprise. As I was deciding what to do, Katina phoned: "Therese, we are going to Barcelona to teach, then we are doing the Camino."

That's all it took. One phone call for me to know it was time to walk the Camino de Santiago de Compostela.

Pilgrimage taught me about sacrificing the old to welcome the new. It taught me about transformation, about letting the old selves and old ways die, about accepting myself *as I am*, about not 'doing' but 'being' in the world. As I lined myself up with who I knew myself to be I gained clarity about the business products and packages I would offer, about the prices I would charge. I saw The Big Picture.

And then, after the Camino, my teenage self's dream-turned-reality.

When most teenage girls were buying *Dolly* and *Girlfriend* magazines, I was buying *Rolling Stone*, *Archie* comics and business magazines. That is how I got to know this character called Sir Richard Branson. A double-page photo of him on a swing in *Rolling Stone* captivated me. It transmitted something powerful to me, and I became inquisitive about his business achievements and his adventurous character.

After the Camino, a friend who belonged to a business networking group rang to invite me along to their upcoming meeting of high-flying entrepreneurs. Her husband organised these events. I'd never previously been invited because I wasn't *that person*. Then I got the call. Travelling, no income, not even a functioning business at the time, I was invited to zip over to South Africa for a week with Richard Branson at his house for a business retreat. This was the ultimate for me. Vision boarding success. And, in case you're wondering, I had a phenomenal time.

Natural law: Correspondence 6

I share these stories with you for two reasons. The first is to inspire you in some way to recall memories that have come to fruition for you. The next is to illustrate that when it feels like all hell's breaking loose on you, a better option is coming down the track towards you. When one door closes, double doors open. Disruptions and agitations are your wake-up signals that you are dissatisfied with aspects of your life. It is your task to reclaim your life and be on your way.

Transitional Moment

Reclaim Your Life

Put creative time aside this week and make a vision board. Collect old magazines, flyers, brochures and cut out images that you are inspired by and drawn to. Step into the world of wonder and imagination as you create your vision board. Place it somewhere you can easily see it daily.

Recall past events when it felt like all hell's was breaking loose and doors were closing, now list the double doors that opened for all the events you listed above.

Part 3: STEPPING FORWARD

NATURAL LAW
INSPIRED ACTION

7

BEING THE FACE

Every business has infrastructures, visible and non-visible. These infrastructures are the systems that have *intentionally* been put in place to ensure the smooth running of operations. When a dinner party goes off without a hitch, you know it was not by accident but by design. That design is attention to, and commitment to, subtle systems that amplify and exemplify the visible face of the party.

The attention you pay to your infrastructure is the difference between a public face of ease and professionalism – and chaos and insecurity. Which kind of practice would you trust with your health and wellbeing? Stable infrastructure, visible and non-visible, guides your clients to and from your practice space, with respect for personal boundaries. This is just as important for your client as it is for you as their practitioner.

There is a third infrastructure: as well as visible and non-visible, there is *invisible*. *Chapter 7: Being the face* makes visible the infrastructures that are important to your service and practice, thus avoiding the nightmare of invisible to non-existent infrastructures. These are the systems you need to map out, display and make visible your services and products, avoiding the chaos of invisible and non-existent systems. Well-mapped out visible and non-visible infrastructures keep practitioner in-securities at bay. I've learned the hard way that if services and products infrastructure is invisible to non-existent, practitioner insecurities will rise.

Invisible infrastructure contributes to poor clinic practices. It leads to apologies, overtime treatments and too-generous discounts, all of which rob you of your momentum, energy and time. Invisible infrastructure is costly: to your business, to your clients and to *you*.

Previous chapters have tended to *you* as practitioner and businesswoman. This chapter turns our attentions to the practice of running your practice, to the systems you must put in place to keep the show running. Chapter 5 went some way towards addressing financial systems, with the introduction of the Money Distribution Process. We now turn our attention to other systems that are inescapable for a practitioner.

Understanding your products and services systems means first and foremost paying close attention to the *in*visible systems on stand-by to undermine you. These include:

○ insecurities about naming your price
○ running over time in your sessions
○ working outside set clinic hours
○ being unclear about your products and services.

The fact is *you* are the face of your practice – your clients will follow your lead.

@

The 3Ds
The Third D: Delivery

It's time to show up. It's time to put your best foot forward and deliver on your promise to yourself and the world. All of what has gone before now converges in Delivery. This is your time.

Put your best foot forward and start taking small steps of action. Step by step. You cannot get the steps wrong. You simply have to take the initial step. One step followed by another step, have some rest, then take the next step and the next step.

By now you have a solid foundation for managing your money and your time. Now you will learn the practice fundamentals of pricing and session timings.

Charging a fair price

It is essential that practitioners understand their products and services, and charge fair prices. Definition of a fair price: one that sits squarely with you and your clients. Finding your price is a lot like Goldilocks trying out the bears' beds. You want a price that is not too soft (for you), not too hard (for your clients), and just right – for everyone. Addressing how much to charge early will go a long way towards mitigating potential insecurities before they rise.

As a student in 2007, I heard of the 'box on the wall' payment system. It meant clients could choose the amount they wished to pay for the service they had received, by putting cash in the box. Think of it like a donation box. This was, and is, a highly philosophical concept. One of my teachers ran a 'box on the wall' practice, to ensure all income levels had access to her work. Rather than give discounts to clients she presumed could not afford to pay her set fees, she allowed clients to pay what they could afford. For a while she had a whole family of four coming in for regular treatments. She presumed they could not afford her fees, so instead of offering a discount she proposed they give what they could afford. The family paid triple the amount that she normally charged for each family member. My teacher realised two things: that the value of her treatment to this family was higher than she rated her own value – and that she had made huge assumptions about what they could and could not afford.

During the first year I was in home-based practice, I implemented the 'box on the wall' system. I was wanting to make sure I charged fair prices, and thought the box would give me an idea of what people thought the value of my service was. The fact was, as noble as this concept is, it was not congruent with my values. I was, after all, allowing people who were likely to be struggling financially to assess my worth. As well, I found clients were beginning to disrespect my services and believed I owed them discounts. My teacher's experience of her client's paying triple was not the norm. In the end, I ditched the box and learned to get comfortable with a set fee. Instead of outsourcing my value to others, I took responsibility for my price, and consequently everyone was more comfortable.

I'd like to share the following experiences and insights from the 'box on the wall' experience, to give you an idea of the dynamics in play as you learn to set a fair price:

1. I was undervaluing my services: I would receive $200 a treatment from some clients and $80 from others and less than the set fee of $50 from others – it was erratic and I was avoiding responsibility for naming my worth.
2. I was becoming resentful of clients who paid the lower amount: I was beginning to value the clients who paid more highly than those who paid the set fee or less – the situation began to play havoc with my own wellbeing and I started blaming my clients for my inability to set a fee.
3. I was not embodying the philosophical concept that I was practicing. This way of charging for my services was out of alignment with my own values. It was noble, but it was not for me.
4. The payment system was confusing for many clients, and this created an unnecessary friction point in my practice.
5. The payment system disguised my insecurities about having

no idea a) what to charge and b) *how* to charge. How do I
ask for money?

6. I would treat overtime so that they felt they got the value of
what they gave.

Confidence in your billing practices is a gift to you, your practice and your clients. Everyone knows where they stand. When
you walk into Woolworths or Coles to buy a bottle of milk,
do they give you discounts because they feel bad for you? No.
Makes you laugh to think about it. They unapologetically do not
distinguish between their customers. And neither should you.

The urge to undercharge or offer discounts is a common
insecurity amongst practitioners. When I run my Patient Management groups, I ask participant practitioners how many
discounts they give and to whom. The usual response is they
discount pensioners, children, family, and friends.

It is not good practice to offer discounts. If you want to
make services available to people who need help, get involved
with community service projects such as shelters, food distribution for homeless, nursing homes, mission trips or set aside a
full practice day once a quarter to provide free service to the
community, for example on pension day. If your business is not
a charity then don't treat it like a charity.

So how do I decide my fees?

I grew up in the family business. Putting prices on burgers,
chips and kebabs was nerve-racking. I remember puzzling over
whether our prices were too expensive, would people not like
us, would we lose customers – even though I knew Dad had
calculated the costs and settled on fair pricing.

You will recall in Chapter 6 I mentioned listing all the seminars I had attended in my professional development years. I also
calculated the cost of this training, the worth I had been willing
to attribute to these presenters. I also collated data about what

other practices in the area were charging, measured it against my first job in someone else's clinic. From this data –the worth of presenters whose work I valued, the value of my education and training, and local prices – I ascertained my worth and set my prices. Importantly, this process empowered me to stand confidently for my prices.

How did I know people would pay? I didn't. However, my pricing aligned with me, and life has taught me that if I believe in what I'm doing and I deliver on my practice promise, people will be happy to pay.

Return custom is a sure sign that your clients are happy with your services.

But what if I need to put up my prices? Putting up prices can be challenging. I've heard many strategies proposed by practitioners over the years. These include:

- putting up prices around holiday time 'because everyone is spending more'
- putting up prices when interest rates go up
- putting up prices when interest rates go down
- when business is slow.

Here's my suggestion: if you have not increased your prices in two years and your expenses have increased, it is time to put your prices up.

So how do I advise my clients of my price increase? I've learned the best strategy for everything is to be visible and clear. When it's time to put up my prices, I provide three or four weeks' notice and display the upcoming increase on a printed sign at the practice entrance.

For example:

"As of April 2024, prices for consultations will be as follows: Initial Consult $320; standard 15-minute consult $80, long 30-minute consult $160. Thank you. Therese."

As well, I physically point to the sign and verbally let clients know there will be a price increase in a month's time. It is not common practice to notify your client base by email. If you do this: 1) keep it simple and 2) do not apologise. I have seen many practitioners' apologise for their price increases and justify why. Reading these emails makes me cringe, so I'm figuring it would make clients cringe too.

In one of my monthly mentoring groups, on a Zoom call with 12 practitioners, I asked them who would feel comfortable putting up their prices today by 10%. Just one person indicated their willingness to act. The remainder were deeply uncomfortable about price hikes, even those who had not increased their prices in many years.

You are skilled. You are knowledgeable. Your clients expect to pay you your worth. What is your value? You decide.

Oh, you're scared about how to set your price? Yes, it's unnerving. Try this: decide on the fee you'd like to charge. Then, get someone you know to stand in front of you. It might be your kids, your partner, a friend. Now, read the following – over and over until you are comfortable and you can speak it without wanting to die on the inside:

"My standard consultation fee is $70. Would you like to pay by card or cash"? (*Close your mouth till the transaction is complete.*)
"Thank you, here is your receipt."

See? You can do it.

@

Running on time

Reality check: when you give people extra time in their treatment, you are setting them up to expect more, and more, and more of your time. As well, this practice keeps other people waiting. And it drains your energy. And it costs you valuable self time, admin time and strategy time.

Reasons why practitioners go overtime in treatment include:

o the client needed it
o I don't have anyone booked in afterwards so there's plenty of time
o I need to work slowly to make sure I know what I am doing
o I space out my clients so that they get extra time each
o I feel like I'm ripping them off so I give them extra time
o I think that they expect me to give them extra time
o they really like the attention and this makes me feel good about myself
o the client talks a lot, so it makes me go over time.

Practitioners who go over time tend to do so with every patient. Track your timing – running over time is unlikely to be a one-off event. Any and all of the above explanations might simply be a result of not making your offerings visible. If your offerings are visible – and you are still going over time – consider that you may be disrespecting your time *and your client's time.*

Of course, you may also be caught in an insecurity trap – once you extended the treatment time over, you feel the need to deliver the extension in every session. This puts you behind schedule for the next client, so you go over time with them and so on through your day. This results in unspoken awkwardness will rob you of your energy and momentum.

Personal example: in 2017 I was filling in for a chiropractor. The following day, one of their clients complained via email that I had spent just 15 minutes on their treatment, and that they were significantly disappointed. Their usual chiropractor spent at least 30 minutes on their regular treatments. I checked the appointment schedule. The client was booked in for a 15-minute session.

I looked at previous schedules. The client was only ever booked in for 15-minute sessions. I looked at the invoicing. They were only ever charged for 15-minute sessions. The chiropractor I was filling for was not following their own protocol. This put the client and me in an awkward position. I elected to back myself. The booking was for 15 minutes, I had honoured the time allocated, I was unwilling to keep other clients waiting, and I was not willing to exhaust myself by over-servicing.

It takes courage to back yourself. This is why we set our standards and protocols in place prior to engaging with our clients. It's a problem prevention strategy that is in your interests to follow. How do I make sure I keep to my session times? I set a timer for each client as their session begins. For a 15-minute session, I set the timer for 12 minutes. This allows 12 minutes for treatment and three minutes for questions and findings. This is the nature of a 15-minute session.

Then there's the issue of clients who talk a lot. There are clients who talk, that's the nature of the range of human beings who flow through our clinics. I have clients who book in for 15 minutes, then talk the session away while they are on the table. My strategy? I set the timer and let them know they have booked a 15-minute session. If they continue talking, I advise them to consider booking a 30-minute session in future.

Running overtime undervalues your service *and robs the client of their time.* Respect your practice scheduling. Respect *all* your clients. Respect your self – and run on time.

But how do I know how to schedule my clients?

Scheduling is an art. Here is my advice: book your appointments back-to-back. This generates momentum, it fuels your energy (as long as you keep to your set hours), and it helps sustain your focus. It can be draining when clients come in dribs and drabs.

In clinics in the past, I was taught to double-book to create a sense of demand. It's insane. It almost burned me out and I lost clients because I perpetually ran behind schedule.

Here's a cautionary tale: in 2014 I was working part-time in a clinic that was winding up. My shift was 2pm–7pm. It was a slow Thursday. The clinic owner was cutting down on costs and I did not have a receptionist on duty. I had appointments from 2pm–4pm and then nothing. I stayed until 5pm and with no further bookings decided to give myself an early mark. When I returned to the clinic the following morning I was horrified to find a voice mail: "I have an appointment for 6.30pm and the clinic looks closed." There was a 2.5 hour gap in the calendar. I needed to scroll through the online appointment system to see it and this I had not done. The client was, naturally, irate and I did not see them again. I had lost my client. My heart was not in the clinic. I was making silly mistakes.

Big gaps in scheduling drain your energy. Book your clients back-to-back. Respect yourself. Respect your clients. Conserve your energy, preserve your focus.

Set clinic hours

Practitioners often feel obliged to accommodate clients outside set hours. There is a distinction between expanding your hours due to demand versus accommodating the needs/demands of one client. Buckling to the needs of others because you can't say 'no' undermines your confidence and your well-being. It will likely leave you feeling used and perhaps even resentful. As well, a client who can't hear 'these are my hours' is a client who has placed her needs above yours. Everyone has commitments. Everyone has responsibilities. If you find your client base needs different clinic hours, then you have a choice: adapt your clinic hours to your clients or find a different client base.

Your practice hours are your responsibility, not your client's.

The following suggestions will guide you towards establishing systems that make visible your clinic hours.

To keep your insecurities at bay, know which products and services you're offering and when, and display them visibly – on your front door, on the wall inside, on the desk. When your hours are visible, no-one (especially you) is second guessing under pressure.

Your products and services

It is imperative you write down your treatment products and services. Here is a quick exercise. Grab a pen and paper and *write down* your answers to the following, making sure you respond with separate lists for each product or service:

Treatment session name:
What the treatment session includes:
Duration of treatment session:
Fees for this treatment session:
Methods of payment accepted:
Your clinic hours for this treatment session:
Additional notes:

For example:

Treatment session name: initial consult

This treatment session includes: thorough history past and present, examination and chiropractic treatment

Duration of treatment session: 1 hour

Fees for this session: $240

Methods of payment accepted: card, cash, bank transfer

Your clinic hours for this session: Mon–Tues 8am–12noon: Wed 3pm–8pm

Additional notes: claimable via private health.

Here is an example of products and services on display in my clinic:

ART OF CHIROPRACTIC STUDIO

Services
Initial Consult : History, Exam : 1 hour : $200
Standard Consult : Treatment : 15 minutes : $80
Long Consult : Treatment : 30 minutes : $160

Clinic Hours
Monday : 8am – 12pm
Tuesday : 8am – 6pm
Wednesday : 8am – 6pm
Thursday : 8am – 12pm

We accept MasterCard, Visa, Amex and cash
All services are claimable via private health cover

Be creative. And do not underestimate the simplicity of this exercise. It will clarify for you and your client your place in the practice. It will give you certainty about the products and services you provide, as well as when and how much you will be charging for each product and service. You are subconsciously embedding in your mind the products and services you have to offer and you're building the courage to stand by your practice.

Please, print out your products and services. Display them visibly in your practice. You are sharing your offerings with your clients. They will love you for it.

Natural law: Inspired action 7

Visible and non-visible infrastructures are vital to your confidence in your home-based practice venture. *In*visible to non-existent infrastructures will prove the death knell to your practice.

Perhaps you understand more deeply now how I came to set not only my fees, but the standards and protocols I have set in place to support me, my business and my clients. That said, trust me – I have weathered all the storms you are now facing. The following will help you transition to solid business practices to support you and your practice.

Transitional Moment
Invisible to Visible

Do you have set pricing, clearly displayed without offering discounts?

Do you have set clinic hours clearly displayed?

Do you run on schedule? Do you run behind schedule? Do you work overtime on some clients? Explore your clinic time management practices.

8

THE LIGHT OF TRUST

When you work for a corporatised practice your values must be aligned with their values, their scripts and their sales processes. The corporate practice has a brand and your job is to sustain that brand. Inside this system, your clients are a number and the service you offer them is pre-determined. You cannot tailor your services to their needs, and you cannot work according to your own methods. This means you cannot respond openly to complaints. Your job is to protect the brand, not your client and not your reputation.

In your own practice you are free to decide your own modality of practice. You are unrestrained in your capacity to respond to what you perceive to be the best interests of the client. And you can set your own terms of service. Your clients do not have to jump corporate hoops to receive your services. You do not have a quota you have to meet. Most importantly, the barrier between you as a creative skilled practitioner and your client is removed. You are positioned to tailor your services to your client's needs. No longer a number, your client has a name and an enriched, authentic relationship with their practitioner.

Why would potential clients trust you in your practice?

You are working alone, with neither the support nor shelter

of a large practice or business chain. In preparing for your practice it is important to reflect on the advantages of both corporate and private practice. Everything you have read so far in this book has presented to you – without gloss – precisely what will be asked from you as you step forward into practice. This chapter is the last step towards making this decision.

@

Advantages of working for someone else's established corporate versus your own practice

Consider the following list. Make notes about your priorities and give genuine practical thought to the realities of your decision to consider your own practice:

- office, receptionist and admin support are provided for you / the provision of all your support systems is up to you
- little or no financial outlay or responsibility / full financial outlay and responsibility
- branding, marketing and promotion is ready-made / generate your own branding, marketing and promotion
- you're part of a ready-made team, you have an inbuilt professional support network / establish your own professional networks
- you are supported with professional development training / pay for your own training
- walk away when you wish / in it for the long haul
- paid superannuation according to the terms of your contract / your financial future is your responsibility
- no overheads / full responsibility for all overheads
- clear home/work boundaries / your workplace is your home
- client parking spaces are provided / consider clients' parking needs
- challenging personnel / choose your own staff

- existing set practice modalities and techniques / choose your own practice modalities and techniques
- restricted by rosters / set your own schedule
- corporate values, corporate message / your values, your message
- address client concerns according to corporate protocol / address your clients' complaints, concerns and queries in your own way.

It is worth stating, in case it's not obvious yet, that what you gain in independence, self-empowerment, career satisfaction and personal growth comes with full responsibility for the business that is your own practice. This suits some people. It is not for everyone. There is no right or wrong, there is only what is right for you.

Them within me

In all healthy wellness settings, clients and practitioners are participating in a dynamic shared journey. What is experienced by one, will be mirrored in some way in the other. This means your own practice is not truly a solo enterprise. You are sharing the journey with your clients. This can be creative. It's rewarding. It's enlivening. It's humbling. It's self-evolutionising.

Moving from corporate practice to private practice shifts the light of trust. The light shifts from producing to creating, and from self-doubt to self-acknowledgement. The shifting light fosters self-trust, and shifts the weight of corporate conformity to self-accountability.

For me, corporate practice was like working under a blanket of an overbearing shadow. There was no light. When I summoned the courage to stand in the light of my own trust, the shadow lifted. It was then I understood the false sense of security

I experienced in the corporate shadow. For me, it was worth risking everything for the light of my own trust.

It's okay to ask your client to come back

Regardless of the endeavour, people long to perform their best. When the conditions we work in are optimised, performing our best results in connection, peace, freedom, joy, power and a sense of magic in our lives. As a skilled practitioner, you offer your clients the best you have to offer, and you send them on their way feeling a whole lot better than when they walked in. And yet their issues surface again. And again. This can be frustrating, and cause even the most skilled practitioner to doubt their worth.

In my experience, people who run their own practice fear accusations of 'over-servicing' clients. It's imperative – for you and your clients – that you overcome this fear. If you feel your clients need additional visits, tell them. To do otherwise, is to neglect their care for no better reason than your fear of what people may say. Besides, if they don't come to you they will find someone else.

People come to you because they are in pain. They trust you to have the skills they need to help them. Whether that pain is physical, emotional, nutritional or spiritual, they are seeking relief. It is common for practitioners to feel apprehensive about suggesting clients return for additional treatments.

It is your job to trust your insight into your clients' needs. To do otherwise is to compromise your clients' trust in your capabilities. Self-doubt will undermine your evolution and compromise your practice.

Your clients are trusting you – to trust yourself.

Sharing your authentic message

For many years in my home-based practice I worked hard to eliminate the pain experienced by my clients. I felt like I was on a merry-go-round of client needs. Then I realised I was not sharing the *message* of my philosophy of health and healing. Once I began sharing this message with clients, I realised I was giving people guidance for making the changes they needed to make to prevent recurring pain. The result was liberating and enriching, for me and my clients.

An example: a client booked in for treatments over a 12-week period. She presented with chronic abdominal pain, she was an alcoholic who consumed two or three bottles of wine a night with her partner, she chain-smoked about three packets a day, she found socialising challenging, she had no physical touch in her life, had not received so much as a hug from her partner in eight years, and was unable to hold down jobs. In a word, she was a wreck.

I assessed the client and prepared a treatment plan. She told me she could not afford treatment. I calculated an estimate of the money they spent each year on cigarettes and alcohol. It totalled more than $24,000 a year. I did not say anything more.

The client commenced treatment twice a week for 12 weeks. Sometimes she came in irate. On her final session she complained I was not doing my job as a practitioner, that I had not given her the treatment that she had expected. I told her I understood. She left grumbling. My job was done.

Over the course of her treatments, the client volunteered to care for chickens at a chicken rescue house. The client began socialising. The client experienced the reignition of sexual intimacy with her partner. She referred her partner to my clinic. The client attended my full-day Sacred Healing Workshop. Eventually, her abdominal pain was no longer an issue. We were working on a paradigm shift in her life.

I knew the results I could get and the number of sessions that were needed. I also knew my practice message was stepping into new possibilities, as I led my clients into new ways of living they hadn't imagined.

THE LIGHT OF TRUST

I trusted my own light.

@

Natural law: Inspired action 8

The reason I share these experiences with you is I want you to know you are not own your own. I was nervous about stepping into my own practice. I was nervous about sharing what I knew to be true about practice. I'm hoping that by sharing my transitional experiences it will make it easier for you to take those initial steps. I invite you now to take a few moments to overview the advantages and disadvantages of moving forward with running your own clinical practice. In this way you can understand and solidify your choices.

Transitional Moment
Trust

Write down both the advantages and disadvantages for:

(a) working for someone else in an existing practice
(b) opening up your own practice and sharing your authentic message your way.

Write a sentence or four of about your authentic message, include why do you do what you do and how do you do what you do?

Are there situations in which you know you need to trust your own light?

What action do you need to take to inspire trust – in yourself and in the world?

9

SHOWING UP – AGAIN, AND AGAIN, AND AGAIN

Why would you run an authentic clinical practice?

The main benefit of practising in your authentic way is revelation. Through running a clinical practice that expresses you authentically reveals the mystery of who you are to the world. It is a sacred unveiling of your gifts and your offerings. It is mirrored in self-reflection about why you were drawn to practice a natural healing art in the first place. At the heart of this attraction you will find a vibration, a seed, a thread illuminating your original sense that natural modalities are a living expression of your longing for peace and freedom in your work and your life. Think back to the early days. Remember what it felt like finding like-minded people with whom to work and live. Remember the joy, the surge in personal power, and the myriad magic moments you have witnessed and experienced.

This is why you are now drawn to the authentic expression of you and your work in the world.

The more you embody your authenticity and your patterns the more you experience threads of connection, peace, freedom, joy, power and magic open up around you. These aspects have always been there, and, just like a flower opens up to form a bud, its petals expanding, the more you open up the more you will experience these existing elements in your life. It is a monumental step to signify that you are starting to master the present. You are no longer buying into the woes of the past, no longer anxious about the future. Rather, you know you can trust the present moment.

The practitioner who strikes that POSE has the following six elements as her allies: connection, peace, freedom, joy, power, magic:

Connection: imagine being so connected to your desires that you feel interwoven with your practice, your profession, your world. You feel included, connected to the wider community even if you feel you are 'different'.

Peace: making enduring peace with yourself, your practice, your why and your profession, generates a deep sense of peace inside you . This is peace you generate for yourself and others by living and working authentically in the world.

Freedom: when you open up your authentic working space and practice as you were born to practice, there is no overbearing externalised force looming over you. You have the freedom to run around as you want, to schedule holidays as you want, to book appointments as you want, to represent what you want, to no longer commute if it doesn't work for you. You have the freedom to take breaks before you break.

Joy: knowing that you are making your mark in the world is a joy. This is the internal joy of knowing who you are, and the difference you are making. It is the joy of no longer undermining yourself with negative questioning. It is the joy of knowing you have created your authentic space and it is precisely as you need it to be to maximise your offering to the world.

Power: there is a great internal power that comes with the groundedness of voicing you. This is living and working authentically. Your voice, your thoughts, your actions. Working authentically is your starting point for connecting with a great power within you. You are solid, you speak up, you do not wilt, you are sure.

Magic: even though sometimes some things do not make sense, you know life is magical. You know you do not have to figure it all out, you know that things will happen beautifully. When you work in alignment with your authentic self, your clients will begin to call you 'magic lady'.

The interconnectedness of these six vital allies for my clients became apparent when my work translated from my clinic into their world. There was a ripple effect in what I had created and authentically shared. The interconnectedness and translation was confirmed when I began asking my clients what *they* got as a result of us working together. Their reply is always a combination of the six allies of authentic practice.

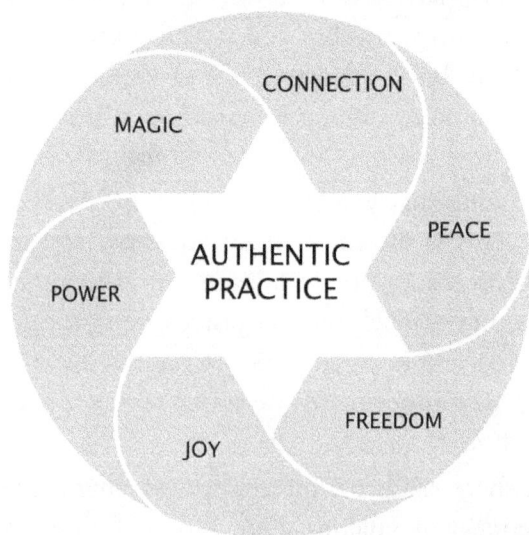

116

Keep going

Sometimes working in your practice may give you what I can only describe as 'head fog'. During the head fog times you will feel stagnant and unmotivated, you may even experience bouts of feeling like a failure — these are the times you want to cry. Other times you will want to throw it all in. You may start comparing yourself with others, and this leads to an urgency to abandon your own authentic practice and go get a job. Yet you've come so far. Are you getting the feeling I am no stranger to these feelings?

As your mind tosses around possible jobs, and perhaps even an entire change of industry, you will eventually realise that you do not want to change industry, nor have you an real desire to apply for new roles, nor do you want to work in an environment of people among whom you do not share common values. I have been there, of course. I know these lines of self-questioning all too well. And how do I know this period of self-doubt is a passing phase for you too? Because you've come this far.

In the midst of your pity party, a small seed *will* spring up from what you thought was barren earth. It may be an intellectually satisfying discussion with a client, or a particularly inspired moment when a client tells you how you have changed their perspective on life. It might be a treating session with a client who turns on the inner lights in you both and suddenly the whole world makes sense, because you are 100% on point with your findings and you *know* you still have much to offer this world. And then perhaps a treatment session will bring you to tears, as the boundaries blur and you see your client as they are seeing you and you step into sacred trust, bearing witness to a journey of wonder and discovery that mirrors your own practice journey. At these moments you remember that wonder and discovery yet lie in wait for you on the road ahead.

Your journey is not done. It was a hard patch on the road,

that's all. It will pass. It always passes. Your task is to show up –
again, and again, and again.

Keep going.

Daily in your authentic practice you will be calibrating
yourself to the path you have chosen. You will start reminiscing
about the beauty of the opportunity you have created. Allow
this beauty to permeate and infuse you. Your own practice is
your giant leap forward. It is also your 20 steps backwards and
your bouts with stagnation. This is authentic practice and it is
just like a pilgrimage. Your task is not to throw it in because it
got hard. Your task is to see it through to its natural destination.

It is your daily duty to remember why you opened your own
authentic practice. Here's why I opened my authentic practice:
because I sensed the bigger picture and learned to see the bigger picture, and because I was longing to navigate spaces most
people do not see or sense. As authentic practitioners it is our
daily duty to celebrate our authentic practice even when it's
exhausting us – although be sure to remember, those early signs
of exhaustion and burnout are surefire signals that it's time to
recalibrate, to choose again, and choose your authentic practice
every time. This is the path of liberation and the inner freedom.
It is incomparable to giving your life to a system that is mis-
aligned with who you know yourself to be. Your challenging
patches are your signal that the time is right for you to evolve
your practice and your message, *and you*. This book has provided
you with the tools you need to keep going. Revisit them often.

Your practice is your path.

@

EPILOGUE

Hello dear reader,

What a pleasure is has been to share this journey with you. We are magically connected, all of us; none of us different from each other. We all have our place in the scheme of things, an essential offering to our world. This is a humbling moment of connectedness for me. When we create moments to speak our truth, as I have done through the writing of this book, we draw courage to show ourselves and our message to the world. The experience is priceless, and it is a pleasure to share this journey with you.

This place of connectedness is euphoric, euphoria that is ours for the sharing, and yours for the asking. So my message is this: do your bit. If I have inspired you to walk the path that is calling you, I can affirm the more you do your bit, the greater your access to these feelings and the more connected you will feel to the world in which you live. The more you do your bit, the more nourishing your life will be, and this will spill into nourishing the lives of the people around you.

This journey will grow you. You will learn to listen to the quiet voice within. You will learn to trust yourself, to back yourself. You will become your own guide along the unknown path. You will lead others.

You are a leader.

Let your leading light shine in everything you do, including the practice of being you. Gather others to do the same. And with that, go forth. The challenges and the joys will come and go, until challenges are just challenges, a natural bump in the road, an expression of life and soon the stories we tell with bitter heart vanish into the mists of no matter. So, too, your joys, until life becomes a rhythm of satisfaction, regardless of the highs and lows, the shadows and delights, that lie on the path ahead. Shadow or joy, a gift either way.

This is mastery. Self-mastery. And as your own authentic practice journey unfolds, remember this: you are lucky to be here, and I am lucky to be here with you.

You are magic.
We are magic.

With love and magic
Therese
www.drtherese.com.au
www.artofchiropractic.com.au

ACKNOWLEDGEMENTS

I could have not written this book alone and I did not write this book alone.

This book exists because of the unique interactions, wisdom and perspectives of the incredible practitioners, clients, friends, teachers and mentors I've encountered along the way. To my many teachers, mentors and coaches across various fields, friends, and to my clients who have shaped my understanding of life, business, and practice—this book is because of you. To all the practitioners who with their heart are out to help people, you inspire me and teach me daily.

To the many wonderful individuals who have attended my workshops. All of this is because of your contribution. You helped me learn.

To my mum and dad, you instilled confidence and curiosity in me through our time working in the shop. Though I didn't appreciate it then, I now see how my upbringing gave me the freedom to think and become who I want to be.

I would like to extend my heartfelt thanks to my sisters, Hermine and Sarine for your support and encouragement throughout this journey. Your belief in me has been a source of inspiration.

To my writing-coach-turned-editor Dr Stephanie Dale. Thank you for taking me on as a client and embracing this project. It delights me that I reached out to you exactly seven years after your sister passed on your contact details. The synchronistic element of the contact makes my heart smile. Darryl, for your patience and explanations in typesetting and Julia for the endless creative book cover options. You both made it easy and fun whilst bringing this project to life.

To Dr Sue Brown, my chiropractic mentor, the predominant influence and contributor to my understanding of chiropractic, geometry, philosophy, all things quantum and how I live in this world. This is all due to your guidance and your spiritual teachings. Thank you for walking the path and teaching many.

Dr Katina Manning, your consistent championing of me and Dr Eric Rubin. You both have taken me under your wing and taught me many things about chiropractic adjusting, interacting with forces, myself and the world. I am lucky to have had the opportunity to learn from you.

Dr Emma Macri, The OG, where it all started. Having the opportunity observing your technical brilliance, fashion and warm heart propelled me forward – thank you.

Thanks to Dr Maria Zuschmann, Dr Rachel Swan and Dr Anna Sallares – the duck slaps, conversations and support consistently elevate me.

To Dr Kittie, Dr Monica, and Dr Sethunya—my heart's family. Family in every way that matters. Thank you for being my constant support.

And finally, to the person who brings beauty, safety, and structure to my life: David, I am at a loss for words (believe it or not). Your trust, love and companionship have brought excitement, magic and fun into my life.

www.ingramcontent.com/pod-product-compliance
Lightning Source LLC
Chambersburg PA
CBHW030525210326
41597CB00013B/1033